November 21, 1998

I hope you
have a good read!
With our love —

Otti & Sylvia

## Advance Praise for T. I. P. S.

*Time-in* is a valuable concept that parents will want to explore as part of their positive parenting repertoire.

**Fran Fearnley**
**Editor-in-Chief, *Today's Parent***

———··•··———

Discipline means teaching children how to succeed in life and Dr. Weininger's book certainly helps parents give their children the tools they need. This book points out the importance of parents spending "time-in" with their children. The home is the first society children are exposed to, where they learn how to understand their feelings, and what is expected of them. This emotional and social foundation is the basis from which children experience future successes at play, school and work. In the preschool years parents have the unique opportunity of developing and nourishing this feeling of success in their children. The information in this book will help them do so.

Using real life stories from every day interactions between parents and children, Dr. Weininger shows parents how to use "time-in" to help their children handle strong emotions. An important part of discipline is achieving a parenting style which promotes secure and accepting family relationships. This book will help parents do so.

**William Sears**
**Co-author of *The Baby Book***

———··•··———

If children do wrong things and their parents send them to their room, some children will not understand why they are in their room. If the parents talked to their children about what upset them, then children would know what the fuss is all about and try not to do wrong things.

**McKenzie Pepler**
**Nine-year-old**

I think that before parents yell at their kids they should try and talk it out. They should start by asking what happened, to understand the problem. Then they should sit beside you and try and understand why it happened, and how you feel. Otherwise you don't learn anything. If you get sent to your room for a time-out you only learn "I'm bad and I've ruined the day for everybody." You feel sad and guilty, and you get really mad. You sometimes don't even know what you did wrong, or if you were misunderstood. Parents shouldn't yell before having a time-in, or use a bad tone, or their child will push them away and they won't be able to talk about the problem.

**Julia Perlis**
**Nine-year-old**

This is a very important and a most helpful book. It is important because it challenges some of our conventional wisdom about child rearing practices. It is helpful because Dr. Weininger offers parents easily applied strategies for dealing with all of the most commonly encountered behavior problems in early childhood.

**From the "Foreword" by**
**David Elkind**
**Author of *The Hurried Child***

*To McKenzie and Cody*
*My Grandchildren*

# T. I. P. S.

## TIME-IN PARENTING STRATEGIES

Otto Weininger, Ph.D.

Foreword by *David Elkind*

*esf* **PUBLISHERS**

BINGHAMTON & CLUJ

Published in the USA by
*esf* PUBLISHERS
1 Marine Midland Plaza
Binghamton, New York 13901
www.tier.net/esfpub/

First edition published 1998

Cover illustration — *Field with Marguerites* (Fragment)
by Ion Ţuculescu (1910-1962).

Text set in Stempel Garamond 9.5 pt.
Designed and produced by *esf* Publishers,
Binghamton, New York.
Printed and bound in the United States of America.

ISBN 1 883881 35 8

# CONTENTS

# FOREWORD

This is a very important and a most helpful book. It is important because it challenges some of our conventional wisdom about child rearing practices. It is helpful because Dr. Weininger offers parents easily applied strategies for dealing with all of the most commonly encountered behavior problems in early childhood.

What is so refreshing about this book is that it demonstrates, over and over again, that our conventional wisdom about the value of "time-outs" is misguided. Sending a child who has misbehaved to his or her room, or to sit in a corner presupposes that the child will use this time to reflect — and think better of — his or her misdeed. Yet, as Dr. Weininger makes clear, this presupposes a level of cognitive reflection that is far beyond a young child's ability. Time-outs do not teach children anything, other than perhaps, that their parents are pushing them away just when the young child needs them the most.

It is that wonderful insight that informs this book and makes it so different from so many other parenting manuals. Dr. Weininger knows young children and understands that their behavior often results from feelings that they themselves do not understand and over which they have little control. At this age children need parents, or other adults, to teach them about their feelings and model ways of handling them. That is the rational for Dr. Weininger's "time-in" strategies. When young children "misbehave" we help them best by being with them and assisting them in gaining mastery over the feelings that occasioned their behavior. This means we have to resist venting our own feelings by giving the child a time-out. Put simply, Dr. Weininger's philosophy is that "time-outs" are for parents, while "time-ins" are for children.

What Dr. Weininger suggests to parents is that they help children who are angry, unhappy, wilful or upset, by sharing their own emotional control with the child. If the parent doesn't get upset at the child's behavior, if the parent sits with the child and verbalizes the child's feelings, the child is both comforted and given a sense of control. What children learn in such "time-ins," is that parents are not afraid of their emotions and know how to handle them. This is wonderfully reassuring to the child who is given the sense that he or she can master the emotions as well. It gives children a wonderful feeling of self confidence and security. Although more demanding than "time-outs," "time-ins" are likely, for example, to handle adolescence better than children who have been reared on "time-outs."

Of the many gifts in this book, and there are many, perhaps the greatest is Dr. Weininger's insights into the thoughts and feelings of the young child. As he shows us the world from the child's perspective we gain a fresh understanding of how young children see our behavior, and what they learn from it. It is when we come to look at "time-outs" from the child's view point, rather than our own, that we fully understand their folly. It is also when we look at "time-ins" from the child's view point that we can fully appreciate their full value.

Dr. Weininger has done young children, and their parents, a very great service with this book. It deserves to be widely read and heeded.

David Elkind
Author of *The Hurried Child*

# PREFACE

When I decided to write a small book about children for parents, I realized that although a lot of what I wanted to do sounded like "common sense" some of it sounded heretical in today's world. Looking at the array of "how to" books available for parents in major bookstores in every mall in the country, I wondered why I felt there needed to be another one and what the reaction would be to a book that asked for more time and thoughtfulness from parents. Parents seem to be bombarded with information, much of it contradictory. If the "experts" cannot agree, how are parents to know what to do?

This book is actually variations on a single theme — that infants and young children develop to their greatest potential when they have parents available who are able and willing to be thoughtfully "there" physically and emotionally. While this may at first be perceived as yet another demand on the lives of the parents, I feel that in the long term, as the child develops, parents will be rewarded with the peace of mind that comes from feeling proud of children who are doing their best.

I have tried to avoid jargon and to concentrate on giving examples from my life and work with patients, families and friends. I hope this book is not perceived as "against" anything (women's rights, day-care, etc.) but more as "for" the creation of a positive experience for all of our children. Having said this, I do feel it important to speak out against child rearing techniques that are widely taught by "experts" and have negative effects and consequences upon children. At least parents should have the opportunity to hear "the other side" and then to make up their own mind. The punishment or control technique called "time-out" is essentially antithetical to the view expressed in this book and as an alternative I offer the term "time-in." My children will be the first to say that I have not always met the ideal that emerges from these pages. However, I have tried to learn from my experiences with my own children and the young families with whom I have worked so that my "mistakes" could lead to something positive — for myself and for others who may read this book.

Otto Weininger, Ph.D.
Professor

# Introduction

# About this Book

Time-In Parenting Strategies, or **T. I. P. S.**, is a book about the heart and soul of parenting — those moments of every day, and episodes of every age and stage, when children are "out-of control," defiant or overwhelmed by strong emotions, and parents are feeling frustrated and bewildered.

This is a book for ordinary and "good-enough" parents who have tried to establish consistent and age-appropriate routines and expectations for their children, who have loving and nurturing homes and who manage pretty well with their children in a variety of situations, yet, who are confounded by babies who don't sleep through the night, toddlers who hit, or clutch toys in playgroups and children who "meltdown" before dinner during "arsenic" hour !

These events are normal and occur in all families — they can be counted on to happen whether triggered by stress, hunger, lack of sleep, changes in routines, developmental milestones or just the time of day. One day it might be the candy at the check-out counter and the next the socks that don't "feel right." How parents and their children react to these daily "ups and downs" will also vary with their personality, mood, health, temperament and those of their children.

Parents care about the long term emotional and intellectual well being of their children. They hope their children will grow up able to experience and express feelings appropriately. Parents would like their children to be empathic and understanding. They hope for initiative, independence and academic excellence. They want their children to be creative and curious, while, exercising of good judgment and self control. Parents strive to nurture self confidence and self worth in their children and themselves.

Parents start thinking about these issues almost as soon as their children are born — and they want to see evidence of emotional development as soon as possible. They worry about "spoiling" and "giving-in" while struggling to make sense of advice to be "consistent" and "predictable." They feel most anxious and beleaguered when they, and their children, become overpowered with intense emotions and difficult behavior — and are most likely to react harshly at these times.

Ironically, parents are on the right track — but often unwittingly act in ways least likely to foster the emotional well being of their children. The foundation for the qualities they long for *is* laid through interactions with their children from the moment of birth. Parents are also "right" that the "out-of-control" episodes present the greatest opportunities for their children to learn self control and grow in self confidence. However, it is not by withdrawing from children in times of emotional crisis, or by disciplining them with a "time-out," that this will come about, but through constant *time-in.*

*Time-In Parenting Strategies* helps parents and other care givers understand how to actively encourage and nurture emotional growth in children by "lending" themselves to their children and by "containing" children's strong emotions during *time-in.* This book makes the link from the colicky infant and the dawdling preschooler, on the one hand, to the resilient and mature young adult that parents imagine their child can be, on the other.

T. I. P. S. is not a parenting manual or a set of techniques to be repeated in formula-like sequence. Rather, it is about a style of parenting that asks for time and presence, and assumes that all parents are able to meet the challenge. It is based on the belief that the quality of parent-child relationships is determined by the nature of parenting behaviors during the times when children are the neediest.

T. I. P. S. is for all ages, all stages and for all manner of problems. It does not offer direct advice on modifying behavior but will, when understood and applied, most certainly, have a dramatic effect on the behavior of parents, teachers, child care workers and children.

A book with "Time-in" in the title will almost certainly raise questions about "time-out" — a widely used disciplinary and punishment technique promoted extensively by teachers, child care professionals and "parenting experts" to alter behavior in children. In fact, some parents have been using "time-out" routinely for the kinds of situations and experiences this book describes.

**T. I. P. S.** lays out the faulty assumptions behind "time-out" and exposes the harm it does. Parents who use "time-out" might temporarily control their children's behavior and suppress the negative emotions of the moment, however, children will feel abandoned and isolated when they most need adult strength and understanding, leading to feelings of anxiety, anger, resentment and worthlessness. Parents will deny themselves opportunities to help and understand their children and will be frustrated and angry when the "emotional growth" they had been expecting is not shown by their children. "Time-out" is bad for children and bad for parents.

Repeated experiences of time-in lead to feelings of competency and satisfaction in both parents and children. The sense of accomplishment and mutuality which occurs after each successful resolution of an emotional crisis lays a hopeful and anticipatory foundation for the next encounter. Both adults and children feel invigorated and nourished by each other. It is as if you can "see and feel" the emotional growth in self esteem.

*Time-in* is good for children and good for parents.

# CHAPTER 1

# ABOUT TIME-IN

## 1. Upset Children and Their Needs

When children are upset, out of control, rude or angry, the very thing they need is to be with a "safe" and "accepting" adult. They need to be with someone who is calm and non-punitive and who can recognize that anyone, at one time or other, can become very upset. They also need someone to help them express these strong feelings appropriately.

Children often experience a time in the day when they cannot contain their feelings and things often burst out inappropriately. They cannot "hold onto" their feelings at these times and they behave badly. It is at just such a time when they need a parent or an adult who can do this holding and containing of their feelings for them. They need their "original containers" that is, their parent who once held them and soothed them when they were upset. Just as an upset baby needs to be picked up and held, "contained" by a safe parent — one who will try to sooth the infant and think about and talk about what is wrong — so too do upset children need this.

They need this from parents, teachers and other care givers. They need this in order to develop the ability to exercise self-control, to take risks of initiative and independence and to become empathic and understanding.

## 2. Time-In

This process of being able to hold and contain the feelings of an upset child by a parent or another adult is called "time-in." The child needs to sit beside the parent, to be the parent's shadow, held by the parent and essentially told, "You're having a very hard time and you really don't know what to do about it. You can't handle this by yourself; I will come and sit with you and when you can, put your hand on my knee. . . ."

This parent lets the child re-establish the original soothing relationship with him or her. Time-in is not a way of spoiling the child, nor is it a way of preventing a sense of independence from developing. Rather it is the only way in which the child can develop a sense of confidence of being able to handle his own upset and difficult feelings. The parent's ability to "loan" the child an adult sense of competence and confidence enables the child to develop his own sense of competence and confidence. If the child can come to the parent in times of distress, then the child will gradually reach the point where he will be able to effectively handle the upset himself.

Parent's willingness to support their children in this way actually gives children the feeling that their mother or father believes they will eventually be able to handle the problem themselves. The readiness, availability and predictability of the parent leads to the expectation that someone will be there in times of crisis. This security enables children to begin to take the risk of handling difficulties. If a problem gets too big, then children know that they can go to their parents and their parents will not be disappointed in them. These are the foundations of self esteem and self confidence.

### 3. Working Out Feelings

Children need to learn how to deal with their own and other people's feelings. They need to learn not to suppress their feelings and not to deny the feelings of others. If provided with opportunities to express feelings safely, children will feel encouraged to work them out, that is, to realize that feelings "don't kill you." As feelings become less frightening, then situations do not have to be avoided where feelings are apt to be felt and expressed.

One afternoon during a car drive with a young woman and her seven-month-old son, she began to talk about the way she felt she could best prepare Joey for the world he was soon going to have to face. She said she wanted to give him the "best foundation" possible to meet up with his future and she recognized the future must include problems as well as successes. She thought she could do this by recognizing that if he reacted to a full bath, she did not need to give him a full bath, she could give him a sponge bath. If he did not seem to like having all his clothes off at one time if she was going to sponge him, she could remove some of his clothes, sponge him and dress or cover him again before taking off some other part of clothing so that he would not have to be fully unclothed and uncomfortable. If he was upset she could hold him and try to comfort him. She could nurse him when he seemed hungry and if he did not nurse for his usual length of time she could tell him that *perhaps* he was not hungry just then, but food would always be available. She could soothe him if he did not seem to want to go to sleep at his usual time. She could be there for him to help him with his upset state, with his uncomfortableness.

She realized as she said all this that she could do this only because she had taken leave from her job and had this time to be with her son to prepare him for the world and its many problems. She felt that while she would not be able to save him from all the troubles he would meet up with, nevertheless, she could give him a good sense of confidence. As well as she was able, she wanted to help him feel that right now his world was predictable and satisfying and that his problems could be solved, at least to the extent that he would once again become comfortable. She did not think that she was "spoiling" him, even though some of her friends were telling her that this would happen. She thought she was giving Joey the foundational competence to cope with difficulties — that if she could be available and flexible, he would have the sense of a good enough world right now, a safe world.

This sensitive young woman thought that her son was able to gain that as an infant and that this sense of competence would enable him to feel confidence in his abilities to deal with future problems as he grew up. He would have a sense of being satisfied, of being understood and he would not have to avoid difficulties. He would have internal resources to draw upon because of the confident experiences he was having. Her baby would have the trust in his capacity to understand his distress and his successes and to meet his needs and desires. Frustration at this time, she felt, would only create a sense that no one understands him and that his uncomfortableness would only continue and get worse. This mother realized that if her son is going to tolerate frustrations, he will do so only gradually. She sensed that he would be able to count on his feeling memories of being understood, and his needs having been satisfied as a baby, during future times of difficultly and frustration.

I think this mother is right because even now, at eight months, her son is able to tolerate frustrations. He can accept her goings and comings easily. He can count on her return. He can accept his inability to do everything he wants to do. His walking experiments are proceeding very well — he has not stopped walking because he falls often. He enjoys eating and eats a lot of what he likes. When he bites something he dislikes, he spits it out and looks at his mother as if to find out what she will do. She smiles and usually says, "We'll try that again later but right now let's have you eat what you like." This mother provides the boundary for him to experience his feelings and desires. Her son is ready for new experiences and he is searching for these — looking for new worlds to challenge him.

"Mother" is gradually becoming a very organized, complete picture for him. He sees her as someone he can trust, someone on whom he can count when he is upset, when he needs understanding, when he wants to play, when he cannot handle a problem or when his feelings are just too difficult. He almost always finds mother there to comfort him. I think this enables him to deal with the fright of not finding her when he needs her, because he has recognized that she never disappears forever. She returns, helps him and comforts him. He is able to let her go more easily now as he is certain she will return. When she leaves and then returns, he smiles and babbles. He has organized her into someone who is a comfort, but also someone who leaves him. Gradually he is able to hold in himself the feelings that she held for him.

Little by little the baby is able to accept himself as separate from his mother because he did have a strong sense of being "at one" with her. He did have a sense of sufficient satisfaction and harmony with her and because of this, is able to let her go and gradually become separate. He is reaching the point where he can re-create a sense of satisfaction in his mind, like re-creating the sense of closeness and comfort with his mother, when he is in distress. At first, this sense lasts only for a short time, but as he matures it will last for longer and longer and enable him to be an independent, secure child. His mother will know when he needs her, when she has been missing for too long. Her son will cry for her and he will not be easily comforted by anyone else except his father, who has been very involved in this developing sense of himself.

## 4. Talking About It (for Parents)

I think many young children's problems arise because as parents we often do not create opportunities to talk about the many issues that arise during our care giving days. We are very busy, we have so many things to do, we have assignments to complete and schedules to fulfil. This leaves us with little time to sit and try to find out what our children are experiencing and thinking. We think we can "train" children to be good and kind and understanding by telling them what we like and do not like about their behavior. When we are so upset by something that they have done, we send them out of our sight, perhaps because we are afraid we may experience strong feelings and act inappropriately towards them. We may be angry because they challenged our parenting. Or, perhaps we honestly believe that by sending them to their room they will "learn a lesson" and not behave badly again. We expect that the lesson will be learned because when we send them out of "our sight" we think they need us, or if not us, then they miss the activity that is going on, or even the activity that they might have been involved in. We think they will learn the lesson in order to avoid being sent away again in the future.

However, after talking with many children of six, seven, eight, and nine, I have found they usually say sending them to their room just makes them angry and what they do in their room is look out the window, play with their bedroom toys, color in a book, or lie on their bed — sometimes crying, sometimes falling asleep. However, none of the children have said they "think about" what "bad" thing they did. If asked whether they thought about "why" they were sent to their room when they are there, they say "sometimes" and then without further questioning often add that they are "just very mad" and it takes a while to get over this feeling. These children seem typical in their responses. They get over their "mad" feelings but they do not understand why they are sent away other than "dad was angry with me" or "mom said I did a bad thing." As one child of seven said, "It was pretty bad — I kicked my train set because it wouldn't work — I think I broke it so maybe they're mad at me for breaking the train — I don't know." Another child of six said that she always got sent to her bedroom when she yelled at her sister. The young girl added, "I don't care, I like my room — my sister is a real pest." Perhaps the parents of these children would have been better off to ask why these events happened rather than banishing their children.

It's difficult to ask a child why she did something and get an answer. Even adults do not usually answer such questions easily. Often it requires that we talk (calmly) with the child, asking about how she is feeling, about what changed the feelings, and about what she thought before she struck out or broke something. Screaming, "Why did you do that!" is not an effective way to help a child to talk.

I watched a three-year-old girl being carried out of a play park crying, "I don't want to go — I want to stay!" Her mother was heard repeating, "You didn't act properly and we have to go now." I do not think the young child understood what she had done improperly and of course did not understand why she had to leave so forcibly. If she had behaved improperly then perhaps the parent should have recognized that the force with which she carried the child to the sidewalk was considerable and in the child's mind, no doubt, just as improper. I do not think that the child recognized anything other than her mother's anger with her. If the mother is angry, then the child feels she is a bad child, and a bad child has a great deal of trouble becoming a good child. It is very difficult for a bad child to become good, or to make-up to the parent, unless the parent helps.

In one young family I know, the mother had been quite upset for a few weeks. She had been ill with the flu and a cold, and her husband had been working unusually long hours, leaving her alone with her five-year-old son a great deal of the time. As she became more upset, she tried to make sure that meals were on time, the house had some semblance of tidiness, their son was in bed at the right time, he had his bedtime story and the many jobs around the house that were usually attended to by both father and mother were done. She became increasingly distressed and her cold seemed to her to "last forever." As these feelings became a prominent part of mother and son's relationship, the boy became sullen, angry and defiant. When she yelled at him, he yelled at her. When she said he was not behaving properly, he said she was a bad mommy. Neither seemed to be able to relieve the frustration and tension. Of course father's presence would have helped. He, at least, would have done some of the many jobs that needed to be done everyday. But he was at work, and could not be home without jeopardizing his job. The boy's mother tried saying "you go to your room until you can behave properly" and at first he stayed there playing with his toys and seemed to "forget" to come out. Then he simply went to sleep and had to be awakened for dinner. His mother thought he was being defiant by not coming out but it also occurred to her that maybe he couldn't "behave properly" unless something else occurred.

To her credit she realized that the child was "not alone in the house." He was reacting and interacting with her and the way she was feeling was certainly not helpful to regaining a good relationship. She felt that rather than send him to his room, she had better talk to him "pretty straight." She told him that she had a bad cold, something he acknowledged and said he was sad about. She also said that she was upset because there were a lot of things to do and he added that he could help. She then said she became angry too easily and he said he got angry also and that he was angry when she got angry.

Together they decided that he could help with some of the jobs around the house. After spending a week doing things like dusting, carpet sweeping, cleaning the bathroom and helping to pick vegetables and cook, there was a decided change in both of them. Interestingly, he made sandwiches for her — a special lettuce sandwich. He washed the lettuce, put it between two slices of bread, patted the sandwich and carefully gave it to her and watched her as she ate every bit of that dry sandwich. He watched her with great pleasure and satisfaction. He was finally able to do something which could "make her feel better," things which he felt would make her less upset. It was not just a matter of making her less angry with him. It was more that he needed her to feel better and to be able to help her in this process. As her child, he had the impression that *his bad behavior had made her ill* and there was nothing initially happening between them that made him think differently. He imagined he was the cause of her upset and he was not able to do anything about this. Feeling guilty about hurting his mother and powerless to fix it, perhaps by a frantic kind of anger he had felt he could make all this "bad" disappear. It's almost like tightly closing your eyes imagining that whatever the problem is will simply go away — something adults are known to do on occasion.

This boy needed his mother's help to be able to do the very thing that would make their relationship return to the usual good and effective one they had. With her help, his doing things that were "jobs" and feeding her, he now felt that he was good, that he could make bad things turn good — something that would never have happened if he was alone in his room, even if he cleaned up his room. Even if his mother said that keeping his room neat was a big help to her, it was his room and not something that he saw as part of the work that he thought was making her upset, tired and angry. It is not possible to know whether he thought that daddy's absence had anything to do with her upset, although it probably did. Certainly no one wanted him to take over father's role. However, what he and his mother did was to allow him to offer some reparation for what he must have imagined was the result of his taking too much from her and that, in his mind, was the cause of her being ill and tired and angry.

## 5. The Positive Effects of Presence

A child's sense of competence, and sense of self, is strengthened by the adult's presence. Rather that just searching for the adult every time he feels ready to "fall apart," the child gradually learns to handle difficulties effectively on his or her own. At first the child may look for the parent, to make sure that he does not "fall apart," so that the sense of self does not deteriorate. However, in time, the parent realizes that their child is handling more and more situations on his own.

This is an aspect of anticipation. The anticipation that the parent will be there when "I need the parent" not only reduces the stress of many events but also changes the perception of situations that could become very difficult. The anticipation of the parent's presence allows the child to deal with increasing difficulties, both in terms of feelings and understanding the complexities of social interactions. Parents' "expected" strength helps children manage more and more problems without becoming so upset that they cannot handle the problems themselves.

Older children, eight- , nine- or ten-year-old, learn they can handle certain events alone. However, they also realize there are some problems they just cannot handle. Children of this age who have experienced time-in come to their parents when they are unable to master a particular problem. They talk to their parents, ask for their help and even ask their parents to come with them to be "supportive" at times in their attempts to handle difficulties.

One ten-year-old who had experienced time-in came to his parents about a problem involving a broken window. He was playing baseball and his throw had missed its mark and broken someone's window. The boy said that he wanted his parent to come with him when he went to talk with the neighbor. He said, "I'll do the talking, I just want you there." The parent agreed to go with the child and as they went to the neighbor's house the boy said, "You used to sit me close to you when I was angry and I could talk to you about how angry I was. I still want to talk and I want you to be near me. It makes me feel better." I think what this boy was saying was that by having his parent available for time-in he had acquired the capacity to deal with difficult and strong feelings of anger or fear. However, the broken window represented a new fear for him and, while he had the confidence to try dealing with it himself, he needed his parent as a time-in reminder while he did.

In a second grade classroom, the teacher had devised an unusual way of handling the beginnings of social and emotional problems. She had a finger-exerciser — a round object with protrusions that could be pushed in. She would give the exerciser to children when she noticed they were becoming upset, having difficulties with another child or simply becoming bored with their work. The teacher managed to tell the class that she had several of these finger-exercisers and she talked about how important they were to her. She was able to give the children a sense of her "feelings" towards these objects. She had a few of them, each a different color. She told the children how she used them and how they strengthened her fingers to do the work she wanted to do, in this case how her "drawing" was helped by strong fingers. She told the children she noticed that her fingers did not get as tired after she had been using these exercisers. She built up the sense of the importance of this thing to her, that it helped her and that she was going to "loan" this to children in her class at different times when she thought it was appropriate or, when one of them thought they wanted, or needed, to use it. She added to this, a stopwatch so the children could count the number of finger-pressings in a five-minute or ten-minute period.

When she saw that some children were "in trouble," or about to "get into trouble," she passed this finger-exerciser and the stopwatch to them and suggested they could do that activity for a short while — "maybe two or three five-minute tries."

The children accepted this activity and their anger, or upset feelings were calmed. The classroom morale increased and the teacher noted that she was not using the finger-exerciser nearly as much after a month or so. She noticed that when holiday time was coming around or a big event was about to happen, that the finger-exerciser was used more often.

I think that the teacher offered the children something that was important to her. In effect, she loaned them her strength, saying that she had confidence in them and that they did not have to "blow-up." Rather they could "work off" their feelings. Very interestingly, rather than "bury" their feelings, the children were able to talk to the teacher about *how they felt*. After a few minutes with the finger-exerciser, the children would usually go to the teacher to tell her how they felt before and that now they could continue with their work. The children were having a time-in with an object that was important to the teacher and was felt by the children to be a part of the teacher.

# CHAPTER 2

# ABOUT THE FEELINGS OF CHILDREN

## 6. Coping with Feelings

Children experience and express all sorts of feelings, often power-fully sensed and expressed as anger, hate, guilt, love, sadness and curiosity. One of the tasks of growing up is to learn how to deal effectively with such passing emotional storms. These are very powerful inner experiences to try to understand at any age and while upset and alone in a room, young children cannot learn how to do this by themselves. Not yet having the emotional resources to both experience and think about their feelings, when alone, these feelings can become overwhelming. Young children need an adult to help them understand what is "going on inside." Forced to attempt to deal with such strong feelings alone and away from adult support, a child may become physically ill, or unusually withdrawn — with either response being potentially damaging to emotional development.

Social growth involves rivalry, jealousy, greed and envy. All these aspects of growth have problems associated with them. The way we handle these difficult feelings with time-in will enable children to recapture the acceptance and understanding we have for their difficult times. Sending children away from us only creates a sense that "no one understands me; no one cares for me." Unfortunately these children will also not care for themselves — they will not think they are worthwhile.

Emotional growth also involves curiosity, love, ambivalence, sadness and guilt. These can be very powerful feelings and may cause children to become as upset as if they were experiencing negative emotions. Children need our support and our understanding to help them recognize what they are feeling, how to handle these feelings, and what to do about them. Our presence and acceptance enables them to realize their worth — we care enough about them to help them through these difficult emotions.

## 7. Winning and Losing

Children can be belligerent, sarcastic, balky or just plain defiant. The only way they can learn about these feelings is to be with an adult who will make it safe enough for them to talk about these feelings and through this, learn alternate ways of expressing themselves.

Jamie is five-year-old and a very oppositional child. If his mother says that he is to do something, Jamie says, "You can't make me," setting off a storm. They fight, and of course Jamie wins — he will not do whatever his mother has asked him to do. His mother becomes angry and Jamie smiles — he won! However, the victory is short-lived because Jamie is punished for winning; he has to go to his room until he "does as he's told." Jamie sits in his room for hours, looking out the window, drawing, and playing with cars. His mother thought that this was not good because Jamie did not seem upset and so now she puts him in a room without his toys or something to do. Jamie cries for a while in his room and mother says to herself, "Now he knows I mean business." What she means is "Now I'm in control!" Soon this feeling also fades; she finds that Jamie just falls asleep.

In desperation Jamie's mother telephoned me for a consultation to talk about what was happening. I suggested that she not put Jamie in time-out, rather she begin to have time-in sessions with him. After explaining time-in and trying to answer all her criticisms about this method, she accepted the idea of "trying it for a while" saying that "anyway — nothing else is working."

It was surprising to Jamie to not go through another fight for control, nor to be told to "go to your room." This time he and his mother sat down and she quietly held his hands and talked about the distress he must be experiencing. Within a few minutes, she was quite surprised to find that this "calmed them both." They could smile at each other "as though there wasn't a care in the world." She told him that she became upset when he was nasty and that there must be a reason he felt this way. Jamie could answer by saying that when he wanted to do something he "knows" she will stop him. When his mother indicated that she would not always stop him, only when it was dangerous, and that at other times she might even be able to help him, Jamie relaxed. He "tried on" this new approach immediately by asking to do something "ridiculous."

When his mother called again, we discussed Jamie's attempt to "out do" his mother by asking for something "ridiculous." Her response now was to smile and say: "That sounds pretty difficult, maybe even impossible, but let's talk about it." She was no longer just categorically rejecting things Jamie presented and Jamie has gradually learned he cannot do everything. He has also learned that he *can* do a lot of things and gradually found that he is "in charge of himself" up to a point. Jamie certainly tested his mother over and over again but within a few months his mother stated emphatically, "He's a changed kid!" When I pointed out, "So are you," she agreed.

## 8. Facing Fear and Disappointment

Children can be frightened or "disappointed," and at such times need time-in with their parents. I do not think any child should be told, "You've got to face your fears and conquer them alone." Young children, and often even older ones, need support and encouragement to gain confidence that they can handle irrational fears.

Teddy, a four-year-old, is terribly frightened of "bugs" and so is his mother. Rather than becoming angry with him for having the same fear as she has, Teddy's mother decided to get picture books of insects, to visit museums where she and her son could see insects and to have an insect box where they could look at "bugs." Teddy was not sent to his room to get over his fear of bugs, rather he is learning how to confront his fear with the support of his mother. At this point he can say that bugs will not bite him, but it is clear that he would rather not meet up with a bug. However, his interest in bugs is present and he is trying to "not be afraid." Time-in with his parents is helping him with this.

When Margit was unhappy and disappointed at losing the high jumping contest, she expressed this by pouting. Both her parents told her that if she did not stop pouting she would have to go to her room. What Margit understood from this was that they also were disappointed in her loss, maybe even angry, and were expressing this by putting her in her bedroom. By not giving Margit an opportunity to express her disappointment in herself, as well as her concern that her parents would not care for her as much because she lost, Margit's parents created a scenario where Margit would have to "keep her feelings to herself." Margit decided that her parents wanted a "smiling idiot" and that is what she would give them. She did not react to sad or happy events; she seemed very bland and did not express any emotions, at least none she thought her parents would not accept. However, she began to fail her fourth grade tests and suddenly to seem quite unable to understand what the teacher was telling her.

Margit did try to give her parents a "smiling idiot." In family therapy meetings with her and her parents, she talked about the sport contest and how she felt. The therapist then helped her parents to give Margit permission to talk to them about her worries and concerns. Margit suggested that it would be better for all of them if she could "just tell them" how she felt and if they would "just listen and stop telling" her how to feel. Fortunately, her parents recognized that at the time of this serious disappointment, it would have been so much wiser to listen to their daughter and not be upset by her failure as if her failure meant their failure. They began to recognize that sending her away from them was not what was needed. On the contrary, she needed to be with them to explore why she had failed, how she felt and what she could do in the future to try to win. Time-in with her parents would have saved Margit and her family considerable anxiety.

## 9. Expressing Sad Feelings

Many parents have considerable difficulty allowing their children to express their sad feelings. These include their feelings of grief and mourning over the loss of a friend, or a family member (including a pet) or even when something that was considered precious is lost, like a scarf or a baseball. Parents sometimes do not recognize the importance of acknowledging their own grief and mourning and try to deny it. It is as if what happened was not very important in their lives. Yet the denial of these feelings creates foundations for an almost life-long sense that "something's missing," something "just feels wrong"; "I don't know how to put it but I feel like a piece of me is missing." These are some of the remarks adults make when they have denied loss.

Loss is a prominent feature in children's lives. They are usually concerned that their parents will be there for them and that they will not be alone. All too often children think that if they are alone, it must be because they have been "bad." Of course, when the parents return, the child is pleased and begins to feel reassured. But even this process takes a while.

Watching a six-month-old baby who had his first separation from his mother in his life, it was clear this was a big event for the baby, and also for the mother. The separation was only a matter of hours, five hours, but after three and a half hours the baby became fretful. While he was very tired, yawning big yawns, he did not fall asleep even though this was his usual sleeping time. He began to look at the adults caring for him, turning away when it seemed he did not get the picture of the mother's face he wanted. Shortly after this he began to whimper and then to cry. When he was picked up and walked he became quieter but this lasted for a short while. Then he looked around at the faces and not finding his mother, began to cry again.

When his mother and father arrived, he turned to look at them, not smiling but with a "wide face" — open eyes, rounded mouth and raised eyebrows. Then he started to cry and his mother who went to take him, stopped just as she was about to lift him and talked quietly to him. She told him she was home, she loved him and that he was safe. She repeated these words for a few seconds and as he calmed, she picked him up and he looked so very pleased. Once again he had his beloved mommy.

By recognizing that her baby was upset and talking to him, rather than just lifting him, this mother was able to give her baby time-in. She enabled her baby to express his feelings directly to her. She did not just try to block them out because they hurt her as well. She enabled her baby to cry, accepted his cry and then held him.

Most parents in similar circumstances will hold their babies immediately. But that is like trying to "keep their baby's emotions away from them," helping the parents to deny these strong feelings. This mother, however, by talking to her baby, essentially recognized the need he had at that moment to have his feelings contained and not denied. This enabled him to respond to his mother without *mixing* feelings of love and anger for her for having left and returned — something he was not emotionally ready to do. His mother held the anger while her baby expressed the love and joy. Later, when more mature, the child will be able to deal with the anger that is always felt when left alone.

## 10. Anger and Greed

Anger is a powerful and often a frightening emotion that all children experience, from the hungry newborn, to the "door slamming" adolescent. Children are angry a lot of the time. Sometimes we know they are angry, when they shout or hit, and sometimes we do not know how angry they are.

Anger is derived from healthy aggression — a life force necessary for our very survival. Without it we would not surmount developmental obstacles, become independent or experience life with vigor and creativity. It can be a sign of health and hope.

All manner of situations evoke anger in children — many of the frustrations of growing, changing and daily living. Learning to walk, starting school, bedtimes and vacations are all examples of events during which children might experience anger. Children show their anger in a variety of ways from hitting or shouting, to dawdling or through misbehavior.

Children may be angry when they feel deprived or needy, even when surrounded by toys. Ironically, children also may be angry when they feel they have "too much," such as on their birthday. They may also be angry as protection when they imagine someone, usually a parent, is angry with them, even if there is no basis in the words or actions of the parent to support this. Anger is a complex emotion for children and for adults. It is especially so for children whose thoughts are normally filled with monsters and other dangerous creatures.

Angry encounters between parents and children are fraught with anticipation and fear of retaliation, and guilt.

Children have not yet learned to distinguish between their own angry thoughts, and the destruction they think they can inflict on their parents through these thoughts, from actual violence to or harmful acts. They feel omnipotent, and this, as well as the omnipotence they believe their parents have, terrifies them. Children worry that their angry thoughts will damage or destroy their parents or that these thoughts will provoke the parents to be angry with them.

When children anticipate anger from parents as a consequence of their own angry feelings they may become even angrier and more misbehaving, even if there is no basis in reality for their perception. They may misinterpret benign parental remarks and behavior as attacks or proof of their "badness." When this happens bewildered parents sometimes end up really getting angry!

It is most tempting to use time-out when children are angry, because their anger stirs up anger we have inside us. As scary as this anger is for us it is even more frightening to the child. We want them, and our anger, in control and "out-of-sight." This is the time when children most need to see that we have not been damaged or destroyed by their rage. They need our calmness and our patience to demonstrate that we will not allow them to damage themselves. We have to lend them our control and our confidence to help them regain control. We have to show them and tell them these things. We have to repeat that we love them, even while they are screaming "I hate you."

A child left alone with rage is not reassured that we, or they, are unharmed. We force them to stifle their original feelings and substitute anxiety, fear and more anger and resentment at us for sending them away. Fear of desertion and of withdrawal of love are more powerful weapons than their instigating rage — no wonder the anger seems to go away so quickly. It has not gone away but merely been superseded by other feelings. It will remain inside and re-emerge in other ways.

Sending children away to get control of their anger perpetuates a feeling of "badness" inside them and leads them to view their parents as "bad." Chances are they were already not feeling very good about themselves before the outburst and the isolation just serves to confirm this in their minds.

It is often confusing to parents to experience anger from children on holidays, special events or birthdays. This anger stems from a feeling children sometimes have that they have taken "too much" from parents who will therefore be angry with them. This is especially true for the child whose parent, even casually, remarks how tired all the work for the party has made him or her feel.

When children feel that they haven't got "enough," and this can happen without regard to the giving nature of the parents, they can be angry with others whom they perceive to have "more" than they do. This often underlies sibling fighting or squabbles about toys at preschool. By staying with children at these times, and supporting their emotions, parents and teachers are, in fact, able to give the children the very thing they desire the most — more of themselves.

Most parents have been told at one time or another that their child "is so good here. We never see a tantrum at school." Children do direct their anger and frustration towards those people who they expect to be close to them, and from whom they need containment. They direct their anger at the person(s) they believe can meet their needs. To send them away for "time-out" can be experienced as a complete failure of understanding by the child.

Parents will also recognize the angry child who refuses comfort or hurls a favorite toy across the room when upset. At these moments children need our quiet physical presence to convert the badness they imagine themselves in us, and in their toys, slowly into goodness, our holding their feelings and our refusing to abandon them.

A very important element when children express anger is their need to set things right, not through an artificial "I'm sorry," but through making or doing something which relieves the intensity and anxiety of the anger. During, or following, time-ins for angry outbursts, it is helpful to share a short and simple task or activity. Reading a story, having a snack, making dinner, doing a puzzle or drawing a picture are all useful strategies for helping children and parents restore their relationship. When children feel that they cannot "set things right" they get even angrier. This will certainly happen if they are sent to their room.

## 11. Avoiding Confusion

The paradox children present to us is that even when they know they are being angry, they feel this anger as an avoidance of being in chaos or confusion. One boy said, "I know what I'm doing even if it's bad." He was saying that it is better to know what you are doing than to become confused. Confusion sets in when the situation or the feelings cannot be dealt with and anger helps to avoid this confusion. As one young girl of eight said, "I can't read the book, I don't know how to read, and, I don't care." She was saying that she is so angry that she is afraid if she read she might find out by reading what it is that she is so angry about.

Children and adults have remarkable ways of avoiding confusion because confusion is so debilitating it is almost devastating. For example, one young man in psychotherapy missed his appointment and when he came for his next session he said he was sure he had met with me. He was sure that we had talked, so sure he misread the calendar by indicating that our meeting day had passed even though it clearly had not. To avoid recognizing his anger with me, he confused not only the day of our meeting but that he and I had "already met." Anger can be so powerful that it can not only make us forget things but also make us "sure" things have happened that have not.

A child can be angry and so avoid this confusion. The anger can feel justified because, as so many children have said, "I should be angry because I was sent to my room." Having been sent to her room, the child feels rejected. She now does not have to "worry" about being rejected — she is. Now her own anger is justified and no longer a threat because she feels she has been rejected already. Now she can almost say, "Because I'm so angry, I don't feel confused. I know I'm angry and I know why."

Illustration by Schultz. Reprinted with kind permission of United Feature Syndicate.
© 1997 United Feature Syndicate, Inc.

# CHAPTER 3

# ABOUT TIME-OUT

## 12. Time-Out

I often hear parents telling their young children "You've been very naughty, you have to go to your room until you behave properly" or "That's a very bad thing that you've done, you must not hit anyone. You go to your room until I call you to come out." Then, I have heard some parents give another version of this "Go to your room" and they have said "We can't allow you to behave in such a rude way; you go to your room and when you think you can behave properly then come back to play." Parents tend to respond to children's refusal to do things the parent's ways, for example, to eat their meal at the right time, to do their homework, to finish their chores before they watch TV, and even, as silly as this might sound, to feel good and be okay.

Too many parents respond to these behaviors in their child as requiring punishment and the most common punishment is "You go to your room and stay there until you learn how to behave." When you think about this it must sound somewhat absurd to the child because it assumes that you learn by yourself, and you do not need others to help you, or it assumes that you already have the "right" way to do things and you go to your room to "tune into" the right way. Again, you do not need anyone to help you to do this.

One might think that the "rude" child who is sent to his room to think about things *would* be able to think about his behavior and, recognizing that it is rude, actually know what to do about it. However, I think children of two, three, four, five, and even six are not able to perform such thinking tasks because they do not yet have the reflective skills to do so.

Sometimes children do amaze us and in our presence tell us that they will "be nice" and not behave like Tom or Suzie. They impress us as they seem to be able to recognize what is not acceptable to us. As a result, we imagine they *can* think about such things when they are by themselves. However, young children need our presence to make the jump from thinking about things out loud while with us, or someone else, to thinking about things alone, let alone being able to translate their thoughts into changed behaviors.

Parents who tell their children to go to their room until they tell them when to come out are actually making an amazing assumption — that *they* "know" how long it will take their children to recognize their faults. Actually, I think that the amount of time a child is left in his room depends upon the guilt and anger *of the parents*. The greater the *anger*, the *longer* the child is in his room — the greater the *guilt* of the parent, the *less* time spent alone.

Telling children to stay in their room as long as they need to or deciding how long they are to remain there are not useful ways of helping children understand the consequences of their actions. This technique does not help children develop a way of judging whether they should or should not do or say a certain thing. "Time-out," as this has been called, is not helpful to young children — rather it is at the service of the parents who, for one reason or another, have to have their child out of sight at that particular time. "Time-out" is actually not a disciplinary method. Rather, it is a punishment that deprives a child of the very relationship that he needs at the time this punishment is given.

## 13. The Need for Punishment

There are so many events that happen in children's lives that parents and caretakers seem to feel that in order for children to develop "effectively," "properly" or even to be "decent persons" they need to be punished. The punishment may take on the form of a verbal scolding, or of depriving the child of something that she likes, or slapping or hitting the child. The punishment which seems to be "politically correct" is to isolate the child by sending her to her bedroom, or to a closet or to the empty basement, or having her stand at the end of the room "not making a sound," staying there until "you are told you can come back to be with us." The parents usually say they will let the child know when she can return. Other parents send a child to her bedroom, telling her to stay there until "you think you can behave properly." Unfortunately, some adults do not tell the child why she is being sent to her room. Even when they do, adults make a remarkable assumption that it is within the child's capacity to correct an "adult viewed wrong" all alone by herself.

Many children with whom I have spoken do not have any idea of why they are being sent to their room and when pressed for an answer usually say "because Mom (or Dad) was mad at me" or "I made them mad" or "They say I'm bad and have to learn my lesson." Essentially, these represent many variations on the theme of making someone angry and being bad. I think it is extremely difficult for children to handle such a major issue of being bad and making others angry all by themselves. Usually when they have gone to their room or the basement to be alone, they tell me that they were playing quietly, that they do not know what to do, that they cry or they think they should be dead. They think they have just become a nuisance, they should be sent away. Again, there is a constant theme of "I'm bad and must be punished."

None of the children I spoke to talked about how they would correct their behavior. They did say "I won't get you mad at me anymore," "I won't take the apple without asking anymore," "I won't wet my pants anymore," and on and on. They identify the problem but they do not know what to do other than say they will not do it anymore.

Of course, this sort of punishment simply asks for just this sort of response. There is certainly no opportunity for the child to think through the issue — she cannot do this by herself. She needs someone, an adult who cares for her, to help her understand what she has done wrong. As the child talks about what has happened, being helped by her parent to describe the event, the child gains the experience of not only realizing parents are people you can talk with, but they are also helpful in clearing up confusion, anxiety and doubts about herself, her social behavior and her acceptability to her parents. This is time-in —

a time when the child has the opportunity of being with parents in times of difficulties, pain, troubles and hurt.

## 14. Happy versus Sad Feelings

It is interesting that when children are experiencing happy feelings we want them to be with us and to share in their happiness with us. We can participate with them when these kind of feelings occur. Why can we not have our children with us when they are unhappy? Is it that we are frightened by these feelings? Do they make us feel like we have been inadequate parents? Is this why we send them away — to their room, from where we expect they emerge quiet and remorseful — when they are really quiet and inwardly angry?

When seven-year-old Lana was sent to her room because she refused to eat her meal, her parents thought that this would "show her who is boss" and "she'd learn to eat her dinner at dinner time." What this time-out did for Lana was make her very resentful of her parents but drove her resentfulness "underground." During her play psychotherapy sessions, Lana said she really "hated" her parents. She said, "they don't know how I feel — they just want me to do things their way, they don't care about my way."

Driving Lana's feelings underground did not help her fussiness at the dinner table. What happened was she would eat her meals at the right time — but about five minutes after finishing her meal she would vomit. Lana was rejecting her parents' control and getting rid of what they gave her. It was her vomiting symptom that brought her into play psychotherapy.

## 15. The Negative Effects of Rejection

When the parent is unavailable, that is when the parent insists on sending the child to his room for a "cooling out time," the child does not experience a sense of parental strength. Such children are more apt to be angry children, even hyper-angry children seeing danger in too many situations and reacting to these with defensive anger. This anger is actually the child's most effective way of stopping himself from becoming dejected, depressed and withdrawn. These "depressive" feelings set in because most children view being sent to "cool-off" as a rejection. They were so bad that they had to be sent away. The anger acts to prevent a sense of depression and in this way is a "good-sign" that the child has not yet given up hope of getting a positive response from the environment.

One parent felt that she had the right answer for situations when her children were "out-of control," that is very bad, disobedient, discourteous or not quiet. She sent them to their bedrooms and locked their doors. She told them that they had to stay in their rooms for a certain length of time and added an alarm clock with the timer set for that period of time. When the alarm rang, she unlocked the door and told them it was now time to come out as long as the children were "prepared to behave properly." This parent soon discovered that she did not have to lock their doors because the children did not come out. Then when the alarm rang, she had to go and get them to come out of their room. Even then they often did not want to leave their rooms. This adult felt she had "conquered" all the children's problems and now they knew they had to behave or go into their rooms. She used the children's desire to stay in the rooms as an indication that now the children knew just how long it took "to feel better and come out." This parent felt that the children had learned something good.

I think the children learned to avoid their mother. Rather than learning how to handle their problems, they had learned how to withdraw in the face of difficulties. I am very concerned about what will happen to these children when they reach adolescence. I predict that they will not stay in their room then; rather, they will run away from home. Home has not been a safe understanding place; it has been a rejecting place without the support and security that children need. These children will be unable to feel that their home will have anything to offer when their needs and feelings are especially intense as they begin to deal with all those difficult issues that emerge at around the time of adolescence.

## 16. How it Feels to be "Sent to Your Room"

I spoke to some young children about being sent to their bedroom when they misbehaved. At first they seemed to say that going to their bedroom was not such a bad idea because they had all their toys there and could play with them. However, one six-year-old girl said that when her parents saw that she was playing with her blocks, they told her she had to sit and think about why she was in her room. Another seven-year -old girl said, "I try to think of what it is and then I become very confused — I don't know what to think about and I seem to just even forget where I am." A boy of seven years added that he knows why he is in his room but he does not care because, "I just do what I want to." Then he said, "They don't care anyway — they just want me to be good all the time."

The three children said that they usually felt sad when they went to their room "that way" but they would get over their sad feeling. They added that being sent to their room was "not a bad idea — it was so we would learn a lesson." Again they mentioned it was not a bad idea and when this was pursued, they said that their parents told them that they were not going to spank them for being bad, they were being sent to their room to learn "to behave properly." I think the term that "it's not a bad idea" came from their attempt to interpret and understand their parents' way of teaching them and that it's better to go to your room than to be spanked.

As they talked about their sense of badness they spoke about becoming better kids, about learning how "to obey your adults." They seemed so concerned about trying to please and on looking at themselves as bad or wrong. Perhaps, in their eyes, they had misbehaved, transgressed some spoken or unspoken law of the family. Nevertheless, sending them to their room was teaching them that aggression or even difficulties are never tolerable. Unless you behave properly all the time, you are not acceptable. I believe that this robs children of the opportunity to explore various potentials of their own intelligence, personality and creativeness. It does not allow children to take risks, to try out something which may not be entirely successful or even to make a mess and be noisy.

## 17. Different Children's Responses to Isolation

Most parents can attest to the different reactions children have to being punished with isolation. One child, accused and sent to her room because she was angry, remains angry. A very different reaction occurs in another child who is sent to her room for being angry and yet becomes docile. The latter child seems to become a much younger child, to regress and behave immaturely. Parents have described reactions like, "She didn't seem to know what time it was even though she could read time." Or, "He started to burp like he did when he was a small baby." Or, "She said she couldn't tie her shoe laces; she needed our help — and she's been tying shoe laces for two years now."

Another reaction that children have when trying to control their angry feelings is to become unusually clean, neat and tidy. They seem to have these streaks of fussiness perhaps when being unusually tidy is their way of trying to make sure order prevails. Since they cannot become angry then the way to avoid disorder and confusion is by being orderly and neat.

Putting a child in isolation, even for a short period of time, does not help the child develop a sense of confidence about how to handle strong feelings. Rather, what this does is tell the child "we cannot tolerate you when you are upset." It does not give the child the opportunity to work through the feelings that are challenging and intense at that moment, forcing the child (who is able) to "sit on" the feelings — suppress, disregard or deny them — but not to "work through" these emotions. A working-through process can only be accomplished with another person who values and trusts that the child has the resources and potential to cope with strong feelings.

# CHAPTER 4

# ABOUT PARENTS

## 18. When Parents Don't Know What to Do

Of course, in some situations parents feel they just cannot handle their children's problems or that they "don't know what to do." I do not think this is an unusual situation for parents to find themselves in. But why send the child away if we do not know what to do? We will not spoil a child if we say, "I'm not sure why you're behaving this way but it sure looks to me like you're upset — so come on sit with me and you and I will help you find out what you're upset about."

A mother had recently returned to work and mornings with her two children, ages five and ten, had become challenging. The youngest child, Kathryn, came crying into her room one morning, just as this mother was getting out of bed, stating that she didn't want to go to school. Explaining to her that she couldn't stay home with her mother just seemed to make Kathryn worse, and her upset escalated into her screaming that she "wasn't going to school, and I have a headache and a stomach ache and no one can make me and I hate you."

The mother was frustrated and perplexed about how to handle this, since telling her daughter that she was going to school, even calmly, seemed only to make Kathryn madder. Instead, she took her daughter into bed with her for a cuddle, despite the time constraints of the morning routine, and told Kathryn how much she loved her, and how much she enjoyed having her as a daughter. As she spoke about how she would be thinking about Kathryn at work, her daughter changed from being stiff and angry to gentle and calm. Kathryn still protested that she was not going to school, and her mother just accepted these statements as expressions of her anger at her mother. After only five minutes Kathryn jumped out of bed and went to get dressed.

Even though this mother initially did not know what to do, by having a time-in with her daughter she was able to contain her daughter's feelings and help her prepare for school. Not having this short time-in with her, and forcing her to get ready for school, would have made it much more difficult for Kathryn. She would not have been able to manage her anger about going to school that morning because she would have experienced another version of the already existing problem — her anger and anxiety associated with her mother's going back to work — a further sense of being alone, a sense that work is more important than her, a sense of not belonging to her mother.

By taking the time to have a time-in, this mother was able to calm her daughter. While the time-in took only five minutes, the upset and anger would have taken much longer to cope with in any other way.

## 19. Seeing Ourselves in Our Children

It is very important that as parents we do not deny that our children are having problems; we need to see our children realistically. However, we are sometimes afraid to recognize our children's problems because they might be interpreted by someone else, or even by ourselves, as our not having been a good enough parent. We see our children as carrying part of ourselves in them and if we have problems we are often unable to realize that our children may have problems too. Seeing parts of ourselves in our children does make us uncomfortable and sometimes angry (or guilty) with ourselves. To prevent these feelings, we may try to deny difficulties in our children.

Often the child's difficulties will escalate to the point where we will not be able to deny the problems. At such times, again because we do not want to deal with the troubles, or because we do not know how to, we may send the child to her room to "cool off." Perhaps this is better than slapping the child, but in the long run it may be as damaging as hitting.

## 20. Denying Our Child is Growing Up

Some parents cannot acknowledge that their child is growing up and the restrictions on this child's behavior do not change. Rather than seeing that bedtimes need to change, or that the clothes the child wears are to be chosen by the child, or that the child needs privacy, this parent insists that the child still needs the same directions, rules and routines as before. This is a child who is not "allowed to grow up." The consequences of this kind of care may be that the child *does not* "grow up" and remains dependent upon his parent for everything — for going to bed, for washing, for dressing, for going out, for having friends, for choosing books, for choosing foods and many more things. This child remains dependent and when he reaches the age of twelve, the parents may balk at such dependency and reverse their directions, saying "you choose, you do it, it's up to you." This may occasion a sense of worthlessness in the child, a sense that somewhere "I went wrong," when the child just cannot make the choice, or make a decision, and is left with a feeling of confusion.

The consequence may be that as this child grows up he will demand that rules, restrictions and routines change. He will want his bedtime changed and if it is not changed, then he will become angry. Sometimes this anger can lead to acting-out with the child becoming very belligerent, if not obnoxious. Somehow, such children are trying to exert their desire for changes but the way they might have to go about it only reinforces the parent view that "they're just not ready for any changes." The situation becomes a vicious cycle, with the parent refusing to change things because their child is not reacting the way they want him to. This parent should talk to his child, choosing one topic, like bedtime, and find out what the child thinks he is ready for.

It is so important to talk and to listen and it is exceptionally important to give the child the time to respond. Too often we answer for the child, we don't give him the time to answer, and when we do this we only make the child feel that his answers are unimportant, or that his thinking is not O.K. — that adults know all the answers and know what the child "should" think and say. The world for such a child becomes a very discouraging place — almost as if there is no room for him.

## 21. Scapegoat "Containers"for the Parents

Some children are the recipient of their parents' troubles. These children are "scapegoats" and punishment for the children's behavior is, in effect, a way such parents have of punishing themselves. It is as if the parent feels "by punishing my child, I'm punishing myself and, just maybe, my trouble will stop!" Of course, this never works: one trouble is substituted for another and the child never gets the feeling of being okay. Punishment by rejection, putting the child in isolation, is a technique that some parents use to put their own troubles in isolation, to reject their troubles. It is an interesting way of handling one's own troubles; problems are given to the child and then the child is punished for having them. This strategy will eventually drive the child away from the parent and the parent will then say, "I did it for your own good," "You wait and see how you treat your own kids," or "Just be good and we'll all be fine."

Scapegoating is damaging as well as ineffective. If we have difficulty accepting our own vulnerability, our own sense of needing to be nurtured and dependent upon someone, then recognizing these needs in our children will only make us feel helpless and uncertain, if not confused. We have to be aware of the times when we are forcing our children to accept parts of us — those emotions and actions that are unacceptable to ourselves. I think we have to learn about our own adult feelings so that we see them in ourselves rather than in our children.

If we are able to do this, and realize that the child continues to need the safety of the adult, then perhaps the best thing to do is to have a time-in for both parent and child. By this I mean the parent should be able to take some time away from whatever he or she is doing and sit with the child in a comfortable chair — both together. Then, the parent might say to the child, "I think both of us lost it; we are both upset; and I think it's best if you and I sit for a while and get ourselves 'together.'" I am not suggesting any great discussions about how both parent and child got into that particular difficulty; rather a short time-in for parent and child where the parent recognizes her or his own need to be quiet and tolerant — of their own feelings as well as those of their child.

To his father, Terry was always a poor loser. Even when he won the game, Terry's father accused him of whining that he should have done better, not actually hearing Terry recount the way he played the game. Terry's father could see so many faults in his son, but the worst one was that his son was a poor loser.

Nevertheless, when his first grade teacher wrote in his report card that "Terry shows excellent sportsmanship qualities, he is fair to other players, follows the rules well and knows how to handle winning or losing," Terry's father was forced to think about his statements and thoughts regarding his son. What he found out was that *he* hated to lose, that *he* would walk away from a game if he felt that he might lose, saying that the rules of the game were "unfair" to him, or that other players "ganged" up on him and made him lose. He actually did not realize that it was himself, not his son, who was the poor loser. He saw his problems in his son and he was criticizing his son for his own problems. His son had become his "scapegoat-container" and protected him from seeing his own problems and faults.

## 22. When Parents are Angry

There are a lot of things that create anger in parents; from trivial and mundane events, such as a torn stocking, to more serious ones, such as divorce or financial stress. Parenting also evokes anger — anger at kids, or feelings of helplessness and inadequacy as parents. This is natural and normal. Parents get angry when kids won't listen, when routines go awry, when children "spoil" good times with bad behavior. Parenting can be difficult, time consuming and often frustrating.

Parents seem to get maddest when their children are really angry — especially when they are "out-of control" angry, hitting or biting another child. Parents prefer not to have to endure tantrums or shrieking. Ironically, the times when children need parents the most are often the times their parents least want to be with them, and are most likely to impose a time-out.

When children bite or hit other children parents react in anger at their children as if they sanctioned or provoked the hitting. Parents are often ashamed and horrified, as if they were personally responsible, and often immediately impose a time-out as if to deny responsibility. They react so as not to be seen by others to sanction the behavior.

Children's rage is viewed as an obstacle to the real and important "problem-solving" that parents want to engage in. In one way they are right: anger does block thinking and learning in children as well as in adults. However, these angry feelings present their own opportunity for learning and have to be adequately resolved before children and parents can talk together. Time-out as a strategy for dealing with anger and for calming down is flawed. Helping children manage their anger by modeling self-control and accepting their angry feelings are more important and effective responses than using time-out or attempting to immediately resolve the problem which precipitated the outburst.

Time-out is a paradoxical and puzzling response to the urgency of the feelings of children that can only be explained by examining the feelings and needs of the parent. Parents who demand that children "calm down" in an emotional crisis are certain to create confusion, anger and even despair in their children. Ordering a screaming toddler to sit quietly in a chair for three minutes is like requiring a shy child to perform as a circus clown! It is the need of the parent to silence the child which prevails, not the needs of the child to be understood, and listened to.

Equally ironic is the parent who sends a furiously upset and angry child for a time-out to calm down. Imagine saying to a sobbing and livid friend who has recently lost a job: "I think you need a time-out. Telephone me when you have composed yourself and can talk rationally." A comment such as, "I'm not going to discuss this with you until you have calmed down" in a heated marital debate is sure to provoke the other spouse to greater anger.

Time-out in situations such as these is a way of avoiding helplessness and fears of being a bad parent. When we see "badness" in our children we want it to go away quickly lest their anger contaminate us and make us "bad" too. After time-out we can all go back to being as nice and rational as we were before the tantrum and thereby avoid our own angry feelings.

Time-in is a way of accepting the helplessness parents and children both feel in the face of out-of-control feelings. It is a way of changing "badness" into "goodness"; theirs, ours, and the anger we create together on days when our needs and moods clash. Angry parents can't parent effectively and their anger can rapidly escalate to yelling and even hitting. Moving quickly to time-in strategies when parents are angry will prevent them from engaging in behaviors that may leave them feeling guilty and remorseful.

Children do not actually cause or create anger in parents and they are not responsible for managing and removing it. Yet, when they are sent to their room parents are really saying "You made me angry. Go away and stop making me mad." Parental anger is frightening to children. They do not necessarily hear or see parents as they really are because in that moment their perception is distorted by their own strong feelings at that time and the way anger has been handled in the past. When parents take time-in they can explain their anger and children can see that neither they, nor their parents, are harmed. A child who is sent away when a parent is angry will be left with a distorted picture of her parent's anger and she will be forced to accept it and take it in to herself. This may prevent the child from taking in any goodness the parent tries to offer after the time-out.

Gerry was a very angry boy. At nine years of age he tried to hurt younger children by hitting or kicking them. He would destroy things his peers were making and would issue threats like: "You're all a bunch of idiots — You can't tell me what to do — You'll see, I'll beat you up if you don't give me some money." His threats were frightening to other children. Gerry did carry through with some of his threats and it was this expression of his feelings that eventually led him into play psychotherapy.

Gerry was a physically abused child. Every time he got upset or angry his parents hit him, telling him to "smarten up" or they would "beat him to a pulp." If he was angry at the playground, his parent would hit him, telling him, "Don't you know you can't be angry at the playground?" His parents hurt him while saying things like this to him. Never did they try to have him sit with them, never did they contain his feelings, never did they give him the confidence that some day he would be able to handle his feelings. Instead, after hitting him, they said, "You go to your room to learn your lesson. I'll tell you when to come out." Angry, Gerry's parents were both essentially saying, "get out of my sight until you behave the way I say not the way I do." Needless to say, Gerry became a bully.

Working with Gerry, his therapist learned that he felt very angry with everyone. He trusted no one and felt everyone was his enemy, or out to get him. He did not think anyone could contain his feelings or be a "safe" person for him — and it took several months before Gerry felt that he could tell his therapist how upset he was and why he could not trust anyone. As he said, "I'd rather be a loner that a loser." A "loser" was one who had trusted and was deceived, as he had been by his parents. Gerry had begun to use other children to contain or represent the unacceptable, "loser" part of himself that he then felt compelled to attack.

Mai told her teacher that she didn't "deserve any high marks" because she is so bad that she has to be sent to her room every day. She told her teacher that she "wants too much and she must be satisfied with much less."

Mai, an eight-year-old, has begun to see herself as someone who is so unworthy that she cannot take goodness from anyone.

## 23. Making Oneself "Happy"

A group of nine-year-olds said that their parents always want them to be happy and unless they were happy their parents would tell them things like: "get with it and get happy"; "get out of my sight and don't come back until you have a smile on your face"; "you have no reason to be unhappy, we take care of everything — your job is to be happy." These children did not think they could be happy all the time. In fact, they thought that was "crazy" and gave example after example of how unhappy their parents were. They said things like, "They aren't always happy — why should we?" Eventually this group of children came to the conclusion that their parents did not want to experience *their own* unhappiness. Perhaps they had enough of their own unhappiness and did not have any energy left over for them. They did not know why this kind of situation should exist. All they really knew was that children created unhappiness for their parents when they were unhappy.

One young girl wondered out loud whether she should leave home because she was sad and added quickly that this idea made her even sadder. None of them knew how to deal with the situation but all the children — all eight of them — realized it was a problem.

I wonder whether the parents of these children are judging their own capacities to be good parents by the happiness of their children; judging themselves to be poor parents if their children are unhappy. Perhaps they are overly concerned by what others will think or reading books that indicate childhood is a simple and happy time with no troubles or problems. However, childhood is certainly not without its troubles and difficulties and hopefully parents will realize that if their child is unhappy, then it is not simply "their fault."

There was a time when parents were just blamed for all their children's problems and parents have been variously advised by "experts": to love them more, be stricter with them, isolate and punish them, ignore them and probably many more things that they "should do" to correct the behavior of their children. This kind of advice always put the emphasis and onus on them, as if the children did not contribute anything to their difficulties.

Certainly children cannot raise themselves. Most people would agree children need loving, caring, nurturing and guiding parents. Without such parents, we probably would have chaos and destruction within a generation. Certainly children cannot live without parents. They simply need them. But they need them also to be able to deal with the difficult and, at times, unusual feelings they have — feelings that are not caused by the parents but feelings which arise in them because of the ways children look at things.

## 24. Coping with Teachers

A short while ago I was talking with a young mother about her child's difficulties. She expressed concern that he should be able to do the right things at school and that he should not get into trouble in the classroom. Her five-year-old had been refusing to do things in the classroom the way everyone else was doing things. He did not want to use crayons, he wanted paint. He did not want the blocks, he wanted to dig in the sand. He did not want to sit and listen to the story that the teacher was recounting, he wanted to play in the doll house. It seemed that whatever the teacher wanted the children to do, he did not want to do. The teacher began to tell him he would have to wait in the hallway until he would do what the other children were doing. In fact, she put him out into the hall every day for a week and then telephoned his mother to let her know that her son was "very difficult." The teacher suggested that perhaps the mother could tell her son to "listen to the teacher or else he'd be spending most of his day out in the hall."

The mother was very upset. She telephoned me for support. As she talked she remembered that when she was a little girl her parents insisted that she go to her room whenever she was a difficult child. She recalled that if she disobeyed or did not obey quickly enough she was sent to her room. She also remembered with much feeling that it was at that time that she thought there must be something very unacceptable about herself as a person. As a child at that time she said she remembered thinking in her mind, "I'm a bad girl and they don't like me to be with them." She was not able to figure out what it was that was wrong with her. She found herself being sent to her room when she did not eat fast enough, when she cried, when she spilled her milk, when she yelled and when she did not pull up her stockings. As she said, "I never knew why I was being sent away — they just said you go to your room and come out when you can be a good girl."

I think that her punishment was quite extreme and agreed with her that she could not know what was wrong and therefore felt that she was unacceptable as a person. What she did learn, however, was to never be angry. She has spent most of her time making sure she is feeling "un-angry." So when the teacher called her, she was upset. She felt that once again she was unacceptable and now as a mother. There must have been something she was not doing that she should be doing because if she had been doing it, her son's behavior would be fine. It was when she began to feel angry that she called for a consultation. She was torn between wanting her son to have a good school experience and her own anger at being told she might "want to do something" so that her son would obey the teacher.

What actually happened was that following this conversation, *she suggested to the teacher* that when she was to announce the next part of the daily routine, she call her son over to her, and holding his hand, make the announcement. At first the boy decided he would do something else, but the teacher, having been primed and accepting of the recommendation, suggested that he stay with her. She suggested to him that changing activities seemed difficult and he had done a fine job at his work but now was the time to move on and she would help him. He balked, but she persisted, and within a few days there were no more problems about changing activities.

I suspect that the boy did not feel like he was good enough to have done a good job with the teacher-directed activity and perhaps wanted to do an activity which he felt would make him good enough. He needed his teacher to tell him that what he had done was okay and acceptable. He also felt, like his mother had felt, that there was something that was unacceptable about himself.

## Chapter 5

## About Families

### 25. "Good Enough" Parents

No parent can ever be perfect for their child; can judge when it is best to feed their child so that he will never feel uncomfortable, know whether they smiled just right for their child, or whether they gave just the right directions and interactions. It is just not possible to do this. What is possible is to just be good enough for *the child*, to be the "good enough parents" Donald Winnicott, the British pediatrician and psychoanalyst, spoke of.

We do not ever know exactly how an individual child sees his parent in each child-parent interaction: Does the child feel that the interaction is good enough or not, and if not, then what happens? Because it is never possible to be what the child imagines the parent to be, there is always going to be some degree of frustration. In fact, I feel some degree of frustration is a good thing because it acts to spur development. This "just enough frustration" can help the child look for new ways to do things, new ways to approach parents and new solutions to difficult problems. What we can aim for as parents is to be good enough that the child will experience just enough frustration to encourage him to go on to explore new and perhaps more effective ways of doing things — including more effective ways of being with his parents.

One child told his parents that unless he sat in the front seat of their car, he wanted to die! This statement came as a shock to them and they were upset, disturbed and immediately worried their six-year-old son was suicidal — a very frightening thought for any parent. As he was forced to sit in the rear seat he began to yell and scream that he wanted to die. When the parents got over the shock, his mother sat beside him in the back seat and asked as calmly as she could, "Do you really want to die?" The boy said, "No." She questioned why he said that and he replied, "If I can't sit in the front seat then I'm very uncomfortable in the back seat." She asked what made him uncomfortable and his answer was surprising — "I'm angry." His mother told him that he should tell his parents that he was angry when he felt angry and not that he wanted to die, that his anger would not damage them, even if they know how angry he is with them.

The parents of this child were responding to things the way they understood them: that their son was safer in the back seat than in the front seat. While they realized he wanted to sit up front, they did not realize the extent of his anger about not being allowed to do so. He could only express this in the ultimate way for him (and us), as a wish to die. This, however, did not make sense to his parents and they needed to help him clarify what it was he was feeling so they and he could understand and then manage the feeling. I think this little boy felt he was not good enough for his parents and that as a consequence he was being pushed into the back. I also think that to him this meant his parents did not really love him. His view of the situation was framed in terms of rejection and he could not then retaliate with his anger. What he would then experience would be death. With the help of loving parents he was able to say he was angry and not have to perceive himself as rejected and not wanted.

Children *imagine* what things mean based upon, or influenced by, their feelings of the moment, and no matter how hard we try to give them information about what is really happening, it is their perception of the situation which matters.

Probably in the future the parents of this little boy will say something like, "We want you to sit beside us but for your safety and because of the law in driving a car, children have to sit in the back seat." At least he can get angry with this requirement and not feel rejected by his parents. The child may feel upset and angry but what his parents are doing will not be the basis of the anger he is feeling at that moment — he can be angry at the restriction and not angry with his parents.

## 26. Parental Control versus Controlling Parents

For children to be "okay," they need to be in an "okay" family and the members of an "okay" family are in tune with each other's need to have time-in. Parents are in charge but being in charge does not mean that parents are in control. Parents can help their children gain a sense of being in charge of themselves in ways that are appropriate for their age and maturity. Parents should be able to offer the child a sense of their own control by pointing out what it is that is difficult for the family and/or the situation, and what could make things easier for everyone. In attempting to gain whatever it is that will make things easier, and it is usually a "better attitude" towards things, little will be accomplished by sending children away when they try to gain a better grasp of themselves. Children gain a better grasp of themselves and a better understanding of what is needed by being close to the parent whenever they are in trouble or in difficulty.

This closeness carries with it the sense of anticipation. The parent is able to anticipate that the child will feel better by being close to him or her and that this support will encourage a more effective identification with parental values and attitudes. Being close to parents, and sensing their expected anticipation is a very powerful motivating force. This helps the child to sense not only that she is safe from her overly-threatening feelings exploding but that her sense of self worth (and growing sense *of independence*) is not taken away or humiliated. With such a relationship, the child has even more "emotional energy" to cope with the stress of her feelings and is more likely to try to do something about the problems.

## 27. Behavior and Relationships

Behavior is shaped by relationships and relationships mean something different to each of us. We all have certain ideas about what other people are like and those ideas usually shape our feelings towards those people. If children imagine that their parents do not want a close relationship with them unless they behave in the "right" way and if they do not they will be sent to their rooms, then they have three choices:

1. They can behave in the right way;
2. They can become very belligerent and nasty, or;
3. They can withdraw and become excessively quiet.

None of these responses are adequate. We all need to learn how our thoughts and ideas about others may be correct or incorrect. We need to learn how to change our thoughts and ideas about others so that we can behave differently with them, perhaps more responsive and accepting. In order to learn this, children need to be able to think and feel and speak within the confines of a safe and secure relationship. To do this they need to have time-in with their parents.


## 28. Internal and External "Signs"

When parents respond to their children and infants in loving and supportive ways, this is taken as *a sign* that becomes lodged, so to speak, in the baby's mind. This sign is an interaction of not only what the parent gives, but also of what the baby is able to accept at that time. If the baby is comfortable, if the baby feels well, then the interaction between the outside sign, given by the parents, and the inside sign, provided by the baby's receptivity, comes closer and closer together even though it will never be a perfect match. There are always some differences between what the baby sees, needs and understands his parents to be "on the inside," and what his parents actually are "on the outside" or "in reality." Parents can never know exactly what their child needs. They do their best to satisfy the child, and yet sometimes the child continues to be upset. The child's inside needs and the parent's outside satisfactions for the need may never match perfectly.

If I am a tired and cranky child, then, even if my parents are soft-spoken and patient, I still feel them, experience them, and interpret them in the way I am. I am uncomfortable and no matter how much they do, I still feel uncomfortable and so to me they are not the giving and nurturing parents I need right now. So I cry and fret and my parents say, "I don't know what to do for you, everything I do is wrong."

It is very important at this point for the parents not to give up. If they continue trying to help the child who is ill or "over tired," even though he does not seem to respond at first, he will soon be asleep. If he has a fever, he falls asleep feeling that his parents are doing something to help him. To give up is to push the interaction between the real (external) sign offered by the parents and the child's perceived internal sign in such a way as to force the internal to become like the external. This is not helpful because at that moment the child's internal sign is that of a "bad parent" because "I still have a fever and feel uncomfortable," and this sign does not offer reassurance at a time when reassurance is needed.

Children make a personal interpretation of whatever we do. They make sense of their experiences on the basis of how the *internal* sign, the internal experience of parents, corresponds to the real parents. The saying about justice having not only to be done but *be perceived as* being done has relevancy here. Conflicts and problems arise for children when parents assume children do not have an internal idea of how they feel. Patient persistence on the part of parents actually enables the children's uncomfortable internal sign to gradually alter towards becoming more in keeping with what the real parent so often actually intends, that is, to be helpful to their distressed child. Although often difficult for us in the short term, because our internal sign is not being perceived accurately by our children, we nevertheless need to help children learn they can expect good through experiencing parental patience, tenderness and more patience. We need to have our own feelings of frustration, powerlessness or hopelessness "held" or appreciated by someone else, perhaps our spouse or our own parents when this is possible.

One adult described having always felt that her parents were cold, unloving and rigid in their relationship with her. She felt that even though they said they were helping her, and from their point of view they were always available to her, this woman felt she had, and still has, an image of her parents as rejecting. She felt that if she were angry, or felt anger, that their love for her would change and they would stop loving her. Her internal parental sign was of cold, rejecting parents, yet her parents told her that they were not such people. She remembers how they gave her a certain number of minutes to feel better so that "everyone could go on doing what they were doing." For this woman, the conflict was the discrepancy between what she felt, what her internal signs told her, and what she was told she should be feeling about her parents.

### 29. A Child's Understanding of "Bad Behavior"

There is always the issue of whether or not the child actually understands what the adult views as bad behavior deserving punishment. It may not even be a matter of having a similar understanding of why the child is to be punished. It may be that the child does not see the parent's point of view and does not agree that he or she has done something wrong. Of course the child may tell her parent that she was allowed to do the very same thing yesterday: "Why can't I do it today and not be punished?" Sometimes the parent responds with, "Today is a different day!" This does not make very much sense to the child who knows that one day is not the same as another day but since things happen that are the same everyday, like meals, then why should she be punished for doing something which was acceptable the day before?

Then the parent may respond that, "I'm tired today and I can't stand that noise." But again, for the child this does not mean that she is a bad person or has done a bad thing. She then either becomes angry with the parent or else she may feel that she has done something unacceptable without knowing what it was, and feels sad. She cannot predict how to maintain a sense of being a good girl because her behavior is rated by her parent's sense of how *they* feel rather than what she is doing.

Certainly none of these situations will be tolerable for the child. Too often the "bad" behavior is punished by isolation "until you behave properly," or by the parent telling the child how "disappointed" they are in how he behaves. Very little is more damaging to a child's sense of self esteem than this. The child just does not know how to behave because the cues are not clear or consistent. She may feel not only confused but also that she just cannot be good and is not acceptable.

A clear, if sad, example of this occurred in a difficult family situation involving a young girl and her mother. This seven- year-old girl had tried to cook. She had awakened early in the morning and her thought was to surprise her mother with a cake that she would make "all by myself." She set out to make this cake "just the same way as my mother does." She had eggs, water, milk, sugar, salt, flour, butter and had mixed an unmeasured amount into a large mixing bowl. She then had cut pieces of bananas into the batter. Next, she turned on the oven. She knew which dial to turn but of course did not realize the temperature she had set for the oven. She placed the mixing bowl with its contents into the oven and there it sat until the bowl broke and the batter flowed all over the bottom of the oven and began to seep out onto the kitchen floor.

By now she was becoming upset and frightened and went to tell her mother what happened. Her mother came rushing into the kitchen and began to yell at her daughter, telling her how "impudent" she was "to think she could make a cake," how "unfeeling" she was to have "made such a mess" that her mother had to clean up, and how "bad and nasty she was because she had done such a terrible thing" that "could have sent the house up in smoke and killed them all." The child was told to get to her room and stay there for the rest of the morning so that her mother could clean up the "mess" and would not hit the daughter. While her daughter sobbed and pleaded, "I wanted to make a cake for you!," she was made to feel like a very bad child who was determined to do bad things. "Nothing like this had happened to the family before" her mother said.

Perhaps if the parent had told her daughter that they would make a cake together as soon as they (together) cleaned up the cake batter, the child would have not only felt closer to an understanding parent but would have been able to feel more like the child that mother loved and so want to be more like mother. The child's self confidence and self esteem would have been increased even though the cake she wanted to make did not work out. However, this was not the case and the girl felt very upset and as someone who did not deserve her mother's love.

## 30. Sense of Responsibility for Parents' Distress

It is almost impossible for a child to be alright if the parents are not feeling well emotionally and/or physically. Children derive their strength from us. They are aware there are times when we are not feeling well or alright. At these times that the child needs to know that it is not his or her fault that the adult is unwell. The parent needs to say something about this like, "I'm not feeling too well today — I have a headache — but I will be well in a short while — I love you and I know that you had nothing to do with my headache." The child needs to reassurance that it was not his fault. I hear parents who say, "Of course it's not the child's fault; of course he (child) knows this." However, my experience does not confirm this. Young children, even six- and seven-year-old, still consider that their "bad thoughts" or "bad behavior" make their mommy or daddy sick.

If the parents do not give the child reassurance, then the child is apt to feel sick or become unusually quiet or angry. Anger is the child's attempt to fight off the bad feeling that, "I am responsible for my daddy's sickness." While this sounds paradoxical, because the parent may seem to become even more upset and/or sick if their child is angry, this child nevertheless persists with this angry behavior, all the while trying to fight off his badness. It is not the child's attempt to get punished; it is not the child's way of saying, "You must hurt me like I hurt you, so punish me." Rather, it is the child's best way to get rid of the bad feeling that he is so certain is causing such pain to his parent. It's like sending the anger "out there" so the child won't have the bad thoughts which are felt to have caused the parental pains.

Another kind of child, the withdrawn child, attempts to pull back to such an extent that he will not pain the parent any longer. This child hides and may even refuse to communicate because he is so certain that any further action on his part will damage the parent all the more. It is as if this child's conscience is working overtime and feels very guilty for what is perceived as his fault. Being this withdrawn is a kind of depression where the child is so certain that he has done something wrong to his parent. Perhaps he has even taken too much from them, and now the parent is suffering. This child imagines that if he withdraws and presents no further problems for his parent, then the illness and/or problem will disappear. In a way, this child thinks that his thoughts and feelings must be so powerful, that they can harm or even destroy others, so best to withdraw.

One little boy of seven, in play psychotherapy, felt he had killed his mother because the day before she died he was so angry with her that he muttered, so that others could hear, "I hope she dies." And then, later, she did die. This child "knew" that his wish had killed his mother. He had been so angry because she was in hospital and not at home where he needed her to be. He was angry because she was gone. She was not there to help him with his special needs, to contain his fear, anxieties and even his anger. She was not available to him; she went somewhere else because she was sick. But the "rub" was he was sure he had made her sick because he had needed her and his need for her had just been too great. That's what put her into the hospital. In this child's mind, he had taken so much from her that she became ill. Then, in his withdrawn state, because she was the only one who could help him and she was not there, his anger could no longer be held back. In his anger he wished her dead and she did die.

The child's remorse was great but very few knew about how he felt. He withdrew and tried to carry on a kind of reparation — his attempt to make up for having caused his mother's death. This first form of reparation was to try to hurt himself. He walked aimlessly into the middle of the traffic and on two occasions was hit by a car. He was not injured seriously but hurt enough to feel pain for several days. The surviving parent did not recognize these "accidents" since the child suffered in silence. Hurting himself did not seem to work and he began to try to make things. In his mind he decided that what he would do was make "nice things" that he would put on the dining room table, hoping that the things he had made would be "taken" by his dead mother.

What he was doing was offering a kind of sacrifice for what he considered to be his bad deeds. The objects he made were usually drawings and collages that he secretly placed on the table before he went to bed. No one was to see him do this and then first thing in the morning he would look to see if his sacrifice was still there. Often it was there but sometimes the table was cleared and his mother's sacrifice was removed. He was sure it went to her. He never looked in the garbage, in fact he refused to have anything to do with garbage. His therapist found this very interesting because if the child had looked in the garbage he might have found his sacrifice there. He told his therapist he never looked, so in his mind it was never there. His sacrifices were removed enough times to make him finally think he had made up for his badness. Of course he never forgot about his wish but in his work in play psychotherapy he gradually understood how unacceptable his angry feelings were to himself and how frightened he was by them. He realized how powerful he thought they were and that he was sure he had killed his mother. He began to understand how he needed her and could not account for her absence in any other way other than to blame himself.

Therapist and child talked about how guilty he felt and how he was so sure no one would ever be able to help him deal with his anger that he withdrew. In play psychotherapy he found a time-in — a time when he could feel safe enough to explore his terrible feelings with someone who did not criticize, judge and certainly did not punish him. In this time-in he could gradually tolerate his own anger and understand why he said and felt what he did. He realized that no one can wish for and cause another's death. "No one is so powerful," he said.

Sometimes children develop various physical illnesses so that they can be in a position where they will not just get the physical attention they need medically, but also be in a position where the adult will protect and nurture them. When a child is ill, the adult keeps the child in bed, sits with him and offers special foods. In these ways, the adult provides time-in for the child. I do not mean that all physical illnesses are caused by scary, bad feelings. However, certainly these scary feelings contribute to actual physical illness and at other times can initiate physical problems. Such problems can be headaches, muscular pains and aches, "sick feelings" and stomach aches. (However, I think it is urgent that every child be medically examined before deciding upon emotions as the cause of the physical problem. Stomach aches are not necessarily always physical in nature, but medical examination is necessary if there are persistent stomach complaints.)

It is kindness, sensitivity, empathy, tolerance, tender care and acceptance that the child gains in time-in with the parent. It is the safety that the parent or another emotionally attuned care giver can provide for the child at those times of intolerable emotional feelings.

## 31. Not Being Able to Do "Anything Right"

Sometimes a child may have the idea that she cannot do anything right, that she is just "no good." Such a child has great difficulty not spoiling everything that she lays her hands on. It is as if she "knows" everything she does will turn wrong because that is what she has been told so often. But it is not just "things" that go wrong; it is basically the relationship between this child and her parents that can "never" go right. She feels that she is responsible for that poor relationship because she has not been told that there is something of "value" in her. This something is what her parents value and keep loving even if there is a problem. When a child does not think that there is *anything she* can do about a problem, then even if she sees she could do something to improve the relationship, she does not. She is so sure it just will not work. As one girl of eight told me, "Anyway nothing has worked."

Children like this may also try to do "nothing" and for them it seems a safe way of being "because if you try to do something then you might do too much. Too many of your feelings will come out and perhaps your feelings will get out of control." If that happens then "you're in for it." It is indeed very frightening for children to not have someone who helps them value themselves by valuing them. It is also very frightening for children, often immobilizing, if they do not have a person who can help them with their feelings by telling them, "I'll help you with that" — essentially taking over for them when things get overwhelming or frightening. Children need adults to be their safe parents, their boundaries, their control when they cannot bring on these controls themselves. The best way to do this is by being beside the child who is in trouble.

## 32. The Good Child

We all know children who at six years seem so much more like sixty years. They are just so good, never "talking back" and always doing things in ways that the parents say are "just the right ways." They go to bed when told, they eat "properly," they do not get into difficulties and generally really seem like wondrous children. Well maybe they are, but my concern is that, in trying to please their parents and be what they imagine their parents expect, they by-pass the ordinary difficulties most children experience in growing up. We all have periods of trouble at some time or another. We cannot escape troubles; just growing up is a trouble because we need things — new things. These children are trying to be too good and too grown up. By doing this they miss out in learning how to deal with developmental problems like how to deal with stresses, competition and frustration. These children do not have the opportunity of working through these problems. They have avoided them by being "too good" at times in their life when they needed to be "difficult."

I know one little boy who, at ten years of age, considered that he was his mother's savior. He was going to protect her from any harm or difficulty and when he could not do this he "knew" that he was bad and felt very guilty. He became physically ill. It was not until he understood that he did not have to be perfect for his mother, by being her savior and protecting her from any dangers he imagined, that he felt well enough not only to challenge both his parents but to misbehave in mild ways — like not coming home immediately after school — coming home "10 minutes late" as he said.

Some children are "too good" because they think their parents will become upset if they have to be "responsible" for them. They want to grow up quickly so they will not be a burden to their parents. They assume growing up quickly means being good, but this also has the result of taking away confidence in asserting the self, taking risks, and being comfortable in new situations, like school. Certainly parents do not have to use time-out for these overly good children. These parents are, however, stumped by their children's lack of confidence. When they encourage their children to try new things, they will always try.

However, these children do not know how to cope with the frustrations of having to do things a few times. They are used to succeeding quickly and in this way showing that they are good. Failing, trying several times means they are bad. With repeated failure, such children withdraw, trying to reestablish the situation when they were "good" and succeeded so quickly.

## 33. Lying and Other Issues

Most parents feel that lies should be punished. What happens when a two-year-old girl with a very full and smelly diaper is asked if she made a bowel movement and she tells her parents that she did not, "but Toto did?" Toto is their pet dog. The parents told her she was lying when they cleaned the diaper and showed her the bm. She again replied, "This's Toto's bm." The parents called to ask whether they should punish her for lying and wondered whether they were being negligent if they let this incident go by. I explained to them that two-year-old children do not "lie" in the adult sense. Rather, they are frightened by the questions adults ask because they, themselves, are not sure about whether they have done the right thing. Children of two do not have any real understanding of the word "lie" — the word just does not mean anything. What does mean something to the child is the emotional tone of the parent. To punish a child for something that she does not understand is, in my way of thinking, abusive.

Instead of telling this little girl that she was wrong, bad or a liar, I suggested that they tell her that the bm was very good and healthy and just the sort of bm that their little girl would be able to make. When the parents tried this, she grinned at this statement but did not reply. However, soon after this incident, she announced that she had made a good, healthy bm! I do not think that this little girl actually understood the terms good or healthy. Rather, the attitude and feeling that was conveyed to her by her parents was that she was a great little girl who was loved and that they were not upset by what she did. With this view of herself, she could then take ownership of herself and her body.

The mother of another child, a two-year-old boy, described what happened when she was talking with another friend in their kitchen in mid-summer about plans to have her son in day-care in the fall. The situation seemed calm, the child was playing with his blocks and the adults were discussing plans. Suddenly the boy came up to his mother and bit her on her breast through her blouse. He had never done this before and his mother was not only shocked but very angry that this had happened especially when, as she said, there was no provocation. Everything was so calm and peaceful, she said, and added, "For him to just bite me like that made me think I was raising a woman-hater!"

I tried to assure her that one such incident does not indicate a woman-hater and also to dissuade her from punishing her son because of the incident. After her son bit her, she had hit him and sent him away "to learn how to behave properly." She felt she had done the right thing to ensure this would never happen again. She did not think that the conversation she was having with her friend was having any effect on the child's behavior.

I pointed out that children do understand some plans. For example, they understand when they are going to go to day- care or school and they understand the statement "my son will be going to day-care in the morning." They understand such statements to mean that they will be alone and their "mommy will not be with them." Again, perhaps it is not so much an understanding of each word as it is the emotional impact that such statements make on children. I talked about children's "big ears" and how even when we do not think children are listening, they are. Sometimes parents use this "big ear" characteristic to let their children know things without actually sitting them down and telling them. No matter what, children listen to their parents conversations and glean what they can as to how to behave, what is going to happen, who is coming to visit, how the parents feel about the visitor, what they expect of their children, and on.

In this case the child understood he was going away — to some place. The parents had not discussed this either in listening range of their child, or directly with him, showing him where he would be going, for how long, where mommy and daddy would be — all sorts of things parents should let their children know. Nothing was said to him about day-care until he heard and listened in on the adult conversation. I explained that I thought the child was upset and angry and now his reaction was direct. He bit her on the breast — the very breast that had fed him seemed to now be turning away from him and hurting him. So he simply hurt it back.

In talking about her son, it was clear he was not a malicious child, not an angry boy but a pleasant, creative, curious and bright child who enjoyed playing with his parents. The biting was a single incident. To punish him for this was to aggravate the child's sense of being rejected, hurt and bad.

I suggested to the mother that she and her child talk about the incident and that she say how surprised she was but she understood that he was angry and hurt, and that he no doubt felt that he was being sent away. I told her that her tone and expression of feeling were very important. The child would need to gain a sense of being wanted and loved not just by the words but by the feelings expressed. This biting behavior has not reoccurred and this mother was able to give her son the sense of being wanted, as he always had felt, and that day-care was another step in growing up, not in being rejected.

Another mother was very upset and disturbed when her four-year-old boy said "use your penis, it works better" after he had just peed in the bushes and she was going to pee in the bushes as well. She told him she has a vagina and in a very defensive way (as she later reported) she said to him, "A vagina is as good as a penis — Girls and women have vaginas and boys and men have penises." The boy was also told not to speak to his mother like that "ever again" and if he did he would be punished.

As this mother began to talk about this incident, she realized not only her own defensiveness, but also the desire on the part of her son that she have "as easy a time peeing as he did." She realized that he was not being "smart" but trying to be helpful. She decided that she and he along with his father would have a talk about "genitals" — but that this time, unlike in an earlier discussion, she would talk about simple things like peeing, rather than on "making babies." Again, a closeness and a simple discussion could clarify a potentially difficult situation for them and make for a family "closeness" that could overcome other problems and difficulties as they arise in the family's development.

## 34. Fathers

Fathers are very important in infants' and babies' lives. But the way I see it, father's first role is as a support to his wife — as someone who tries to make sure that the experience of mother and baby are as free from tension, turmoil and frustration as possible. He helps her to maintain the first relationship with the baby, supports her in doing this, takes direction from her in helping her and the baby, and "moves in" when she needs and asks for help. He does not just "take over"; he does not try to prove he is a better parent than she is. There is no competition for parenting. Gradually he takes on more and more of a role in fathering but usually this acceptance is still under the mother's direction. In other words, he does not usurp her role, he compliments it. He accepts her work with the baby without experiencing jealousy. This is not easy to do for most fathers but something I know fathers can learn.

There are times in a family when father does take over — when he is the primary care giver. Then mother is the supportive person. But in most of my experiences, it has been the mother who is the primary care giver.

In a family I know where father was the primary care giver for the first four years of their son's life, I noticed that the child related very well to both mother and father, and there were no problems that they or I noticed. He got along very well with his peers, he was secure in his relationship to his parents, he entered day-care at three years of age and was not disturbed by the separation experience. He decided that he did not want to go to the day-care the second day after enrolling him and his father had no difficulty allowing his son to stay home with him. It seemed that this boy was doing well "all-around." His very early experiences with father were of the sort where father took on the role of containing his anxieties, of helping him develop at first a oneness with father and then a gradual separation from father. There was the usual swinging back and forth from being separate to being attached but no unusual difficulties were encountered. When he was ill, he went to his father, when he wanted to go to sleep he chose his father at first, but when he was two-year-old he asked for "anybody to put me to sleep."

He was weaned from the breast within the first month. His mother returned to work after three months of staying at home with her son and husband. Instead of her being the supported one, the father was the supported person, as soon as the mother felt well enough to do this job and the boy thrived within this arrangement.

I think that while there is an ongoing relationship with the mother — that probably starts when she realizes she is pregnant, and is deepened when she feels the baby move inside her, — the relationship' strength and love can be transferred to the father when the parents have discussed their plans and have realized what roles they are to both play in rearing their infant. While the father can only imagine the birth process and the breast feeding relationship, he can nevertheless accept the "start" from mother and carry on the strong relationship with her help, and at first, under her direction. Soon he "has" the relationship and mother then supports this by nurturing the two. In the family I know, this worked because neither mother nor father felt threatened nor jealous of each other. Unfortunately, this is not the case in most families where this strong support is lacking. In these families, the relationship with the spouse is not as containing or filled with comfort that is so often needed.

# CHAPTER 6

# ABOUT GROWING UP AND GROWING APART

## 35. Separation

Sending the child away from the parent because the child is having a problem has some major repercussions on the way in which the child is able to separate from the parent. Separation is a very important milestone in every child's development and the way in which this is handled is crucial for future healthy growth. If we demand separation at too early an age we set the stage for problems, for the exacerbation of sleeping problems, for example.

One young baby of nine months was weaned at six months because her mother had to return to work and a sleeping pattern that was not a problem became a very serious problem. In the first few months the baby awoke a few times every night and was nursed back to sleep. Then at six months, she was weaned with the nightly nursings removed and replaced with bottle feedings. The baby responded by refusing to go to bed, howling when she was placed in her crib, refusing to be fed or comforted and falling asleep only because of exhaustion. Her parents called; the mother could not leave her work to feed the baby but the baby was accepting a bottle during the daytime. The nights were the only problem — no one was getting enough sleep. I suggested that they put the baby in their bed, lie beside her and sing to her. If she cried, the parents were to offer her warm cuddles and the opportunity to suck at a bottle while continuing to sing softly to her. The parents were afraid they would fall asleep in their bed with the baby and harm her. I gently pointed out that, while this could happen, I suspected it was their anger at their daughter that was at the root of this worry. I mentioned that they could make a bed roll and offer her a safe spot, a nest, in the bed where she would not roll out and they would meet some resistance should they roll too close to her.

The parents decided to follow these recommendations but only one of them would fall asleep; the other would remain awake. Mother chose to lie down with the baby and follow the recommendations. Within a week the baby's sleep seemed normal enough for the mother to put her back into her own crib. This did not work and she brought her back to her own bed. The parents were afraid that they would spoil their daughter if she slept with them in their bed. They did not seem to understand that as their daughter was able to gain a sense of comfort and satisfaction, she would have enough confidence in her own competency to be able to try sleeping alone in her own crib.

It is only as a result of our sense of confidence that we are able to do things; otherwise we do not. We are not being spoiled, rather what we are doing is gaining a sense of being able to deal with our feelings and it is the relationship between ourselves and our parents which enables us to do this. The better the relationship, the more secure it is, the more effective will the baby be at trying to meet its own needs because the well attached baby can always come back to the parent for comfort if he needs it. This attachment is an extremely powerful aspect of the baby's relationship to the parent — and it should be the kind of attachment which helps the baby desire a sense of independence. Only "securely attached" babies try to become effectively independent. It is because of their sense of security within the relationship to their parent that they are able to explore a sense of separation. So rather than spoiling a baby by helping him fall asleep, we actually enhance the baby's competence at being able to fall asleep alone.

This little girl took three weeks to "settle" her sleep problem, a problem that had continued for at least three months. I think that it was after the parents began to realize how angry they were at being so tired that they were able to provide the safety and boundaries that made their baby feel a secure "reattachment" to the mother. Within this reattachment, the baby was able to develop her own sense of competence to the point where sleeping was no longer a problem.

Another little girl, a three-year-old, seems to have been able to describe in very clear and effective language what I have been trying to say. Her mother reported:

> My three-year-old came back to me a week after I'd told her that she didn't have to copy everything her friend says because she has her own special voice inside her. She must have mulled over this one. Upon reflection she said, "You know mommy, I don't only have Amy Smith (her friend) inside me. I have a part of you and daddy inside me too — it's like you're in my pocket all the time so I can keep you safe, but it's really inside me and it keeps me safe too."

This securely attached little girl feels she has the kind of relationship with her parents that helps her feel safely independent.

## 36. Weaning and a Sense of Loss (in the Mother)

Mothers also realize their own sense of disappointment even if they had planned on weaning their baby at a special age. I think their sense of disappointment is related to their sense of anger at having to give up something that they enjoy and enjoy watching their baby enjoy. Nevertheless, for many mothers there is a deep sense of loss. I think that we respond to loss with anger — the anger that arises from a sense of frustration. The baby is frustrated because there is a change in the way she is comforted and mother is frustrated in her sense of being a nurturing mother. She will have to change her sense of how she is a nurturer for her baby. We usually do this quite automatically as, for example, when we say to ourselves or out loud, "My baby is old enough now to try to drink from a bottle." Or, "She can try new foods now." Or, "I will be going back to work in a few months and have to consider weaning her from the breast."

All these statements and many more indicate the way in which we try to suggest to ourselves that our anger or irritation is not something "real." "It's because the baby is growing up." We seem to want the baby to remain a baby — even though we want the baby to grow and mature! The paradox is clear but at the service of trying to not realize our anger, some mothers, in spite of their attempts to see "this weaning as a good thing," nevertheless express periods of sadness and crying. I think that this is an outward expression of some feeling which is not actually felt but is there — like anger. The mother would rightly say, *"I'm* not angry with the baby" but perhaps she may say that the baby is angry with the loss of the breast. The mother has to give up the comfort and care that the nursing provides — comfort for her and care for the baby. This loss will have to be replaced with another way of providing comfort and care to her developing child. She will have to acknowledge the growth and adapt her mothering to this growing baby. Father, as well, will have to do this same adjustment in his fathering role, but his relationship is not usually as "primal" as that of the mother.

### 37. Weaning and a Sense of Loss (in the Baby)

In the same way that the parents experience the loss, so does the baby. Then, dependent upon the way this loss is handled, few problems need arise. If the parents realize that loss creates irritation and allow for this to be expressed in their baby's behavior and feelings, then the difficulty will soon be overcome and the family will have moved to another "level of maturity." If they do not give themselves and the baby time to experience these changes in feelings, then problems may be maintained for long periods of time and only become more intense as growth continues — because the foundation for difficulties is laid very early in life. Unless these issues and problems are dealt with, the responses become exaggerated and more intense. So a baby who has sleeping problems following weaning may also be the toddler who has toileting difficulties. Having to give up the breast or bottle was difficult and now the child is asked to give up "freedom" of toileting and expected to "toilet" in special places at special times. Again, this is a loss, even though it is not thought of in the same way as the loss of the breast or bottle. Since the first loss was not resolved, the second one will perhaps be fought against as well.

One family I knew were moving and their three children were having a "fit." The parents said the children were angry, balking, irritable and complaining that all their friends were at the old place and they "knew no one at the new place." The three of them, ranging in age from six to ten, were adamant about this move and would raise a daily litany of complaints and reasons why they would not move. In speaking to the parents about the forthcoming move, I spoke about the separation and loss and the resultant anger. They pointed out that the children had no choice in the matter, they just had to move and "that's that!" We discussed this more fully, with the attempt to help them realize that their children felt as if they were losing part of themselves — that "somehow a part of them would stay in the old house and they'd never be able to get it back again." The parents could understand this and said that they would miss the conveniences that they had built into this house but they were going to give it up to get even more conveniences. I pointed out that the children could not see it that way but that perhaps there were some things they could do as a family that might help them cope with this loss and separation. I suggested that each of them take photographs of the house and surroundings "their way" and that they create an album of their "last home." They were also going to transplant some perennial flowers and, if possible, a tree and add, some rocks that each member of the family could choose from their old garden. While the parents were skeptical of this, they did say they would try it and would "talk it up" that evening. The children's response to this was immediate. They liked the idea and set out to decide what they were going to photograph and what part of the garden they would bring to their new house.

I think this recommendation worked for this family. Even though the children were angry about the move, they nevertheless were prepared to try to deal with their loss as long as the parents were able to offer them *something to do* — something to deal with the pain of separation. If the children or adults are not prepared to "deal" with the separation, then more than simple recommendations about what to do are required. A few sessions with the whole family where discussions about loss and separation would be vital so that the past separations and the unresolved loss and anger could be touched upon. This would give a greater opportunity for the individuals to accept that there are some very positive things that can be done to alleviate the anger.

Whenever we can, I think it is important to introduce loss gradually. By loss here, I mean not only weaning, but toileting, going to school, moving house, moving to another school, etc. I think it is important to not only give the adults the chance to think about the change, and the loss of something that is known and recognized, it is equally important that children be given time to get to know how they feel about the impending changes.

If loss and changes are suddenly imposed upon children, then many children will not be able to deal with their subsequent feelings. They either cut off their feelings because there is just too much anxiety to deal with, or they become "problem children" and begin to balk at whatever they are told to do. If we are not given the opportunity to try to settle such feelings then we react to other situations and events the way we reacted to the original change and loss.

As adults, we try to react appropriately to loss and most of the time we do. It is only when there is some really important loss that we then know just how we really feel, and begin to recognize how we really felt about some loss that happened a long time ago when we were children. I am talking about the death of a loved one, where that loss brings on a flood of feelings: sadness, withdrawal and also anger. We cry at the loss of a dear friend and we recall the pain we experienced at the death of our parent.

This anger at the loss of a loved parent or friend may be expressed when we say, "Why did that have to happen? — Why did it happen now just when things were so alright for him or her? Why now? She was enjoying her new apartment so much and she just moved in." These statements not only indicate our bewilderment at the loss but also our anger at the loss. Children react to most situations in this way: "Why do I have to leave the game? — Why can't I stay longer, just when I'm having fun?" I do not mean that leaving the game is the same as death, but rather that our emotions are much stronger than we usually recognize and children's emotions are equally strong but sometimes very hard to understand.

We cannot expect children to react the way we do when moving to a new house. We often do not acknowledge their feelings and the strength of these emotions. Children do feel these changes strongly and they respond in certain ways, often ways we just do not like. We need to allow children to feel upset and angry at times of change and separation and to acknowledge why they feel like they do. We shouldn't say, "You don't have to feel like that, you're a big boy now." Rather, we need to let them know that "we all have these upset feelings but we will all be together and we can talk about the nice things we did at the old house." Parents need to contain their children's anxieties, not dismiss them as nonsense, or hope they will just diminish with time.

## 38. Starting Day-Care

Starting day-care is a very difficult experience for most children. Some parents expect an acceptance of this decision to go to day-care that is beyond the maturity of the child.

It's impossible for a child not to respond to changes in his life, and while the change is not "development" actually, it is an event that the child will have to take into his general being. In other words, he is going to have to integrate the change. To integrate this event, the child will let other developed behavior slip until he has understood and begun to integrate the idea of being separated from his parent, even if it is only being out for a morning or an afternoon. What does not seem like a big event to adults, might be an enormous event from a child's point of view.

Parents get upset and even angry when a child does not seem to accept these new events easily and without turmoil. They seem to feel that their parenting skills have been poor and that someone will think they are not good enough parents — often their own parents. Some parents have actually punished their children with time-out in order to subdue any reaction from their child. As a punishment technique this is senseless since this is the very thing that the child is having trouble with — separating from his home and family.

Of course the child will learn to control his feelings but the cost will be very high. It will be difficult for him to judge how others are feeling towards him. He will not be able to judge their expectations for him because he will have turned away from others. They hurt him for the very feelings that will allow him to understand and be sensitive to others. He will have to "close-down" these feelings because they lead to feeling hurt and rejected. Of course this does not mean that he will be an "emotionally disturbed" child. What it may mean is that an area of development will be limited — the ability to recognize how people feel toward him. He has to limit her need to depend upon adults because they do not seem to understand that at some times he needs them more than at other times.

Social growth and development does not occur all at once. Rather, social growth *includes* the capacity to be dependent upon safe and understanding parents so that one can predict they will be there when needed. That will allow accepting the risk of being alone because children feel they know they can count upon them if and when they need their parents. Social growth includes this sense of independence, and a quality of aggressiveness. The ability to "strike out on your own" takes a certain degree of aggression — positive aggression or "feistiness" — the kind of cockiness you see in babies when they know they have mastered some action. Children will not strike out on their own if they are concerned that their expression of aggression will either not be accepted or will be punished, that is if they are made to feel that they did "too much" on their own. Parents of such children often have difficulty helping their children achieve the very independence they are asking for and such children become very rule-bound, always looking to their parents to make sure that "things" are okay, that they are doing "things" the way parents want them to.

## 39. Leaving Home

One boy of six years, describing his initial camping experience when he was five-year-old, said that he thought that the separation from his family was terrible. He went on to say that he was so sure that in his absence from home everything would go on without him and that he would never be able to catch up to what was going on. He was "missing everything" and if he "stayed away" there would be no place for him. It was not that his parents would not want him to come home but that they would have had "all sorts of experiences" that he was not part of. To him, this meant he was no longer going to be a member of the family.

This boy's feelings were so strong that he tried to run away from the camp and when he was brought back he complained of being ill. He was put in the infirmary and left on his own which made his concerns about being part of a family even worse. He was so sure that he would be forgotten and then, if forgotten by his parents, in his six-year-old mind he would not exist.

This young child was not prepared to be separated from his family. This sense of his position in the family must have been very vague already, leading him to feel as if he did not belong unless he was there all the time. Of course what he was trying to tell the camp counselors by running away and becoming ill was that he was just not prepared to be separated from his family. His sense of being attached to his parents was in jeopardy and he was trying his best to get home so that he could continue to feel like a person.

Separation from parents is always difficult. Some children are more prepared to separate from their parents than others. I think we understand a bit more about how different kinds of separation affect children. Children leave their homes to go to schools and we are aware that some children have difficulty with this separation. But some children also have difficulty when they change schools, even though they might be with the same teacher or children they had been with for the past several months.

One four-year-old girl had moved from one school building to another. Although she had visited the new school on a few occasions, she reacted to being in her new classroom by refusing to come out of the cloakroom. She stayed in this room holding onto her coat for about sixty minutes, refusing either to sit or move. The teacher, whom she knew, visited her several times but the child simply refused to come into the classroom. When she came into the classroom, holding onto her coat, she sat herself right in front of the teacher, looking at her intently. Whenever the teacher had to move, the child looked back at the cloakroom but followed the teacher, trying to remain very close to her.

Another four-year-old boy told his parents that he did not want to go to the "new school" because, he insisted, none of the children he knew would be there. He exclaimed, "The teacher won't be there!" His parents brought him to the class but the ride to school and entering the classroom was a tearful experience for the child. When he finally came into the class, he told his teacher that she had to read the same story that she had read to the class for most of the past week, "A Difficult Day." He remained close to her and insisted that all he could do was play in the sand, saying, "I don't want to play with anybody." He seemed "jumpy" and quite unable to settle, a characteristic that was quite unlike his usual behavior.

Another young boy announced to "the whole school" that his new classroom was not as nice as his old one. The teacher suggested that the new classroom was "much brighter" to which he responded, "It's not as bright as my old classroom." His "old classroom" had been in a basement.

Some children and their parents made a map of the new route that they had taken to get to the new school. They surveyed the area, got the streets going in the right directions, labeled the streets, marked their house, the new school and some significant buildings on route to the new school. The children made sure that they looked at their map several days before the move, and used the map to "help" their parents find the correct streets and the "right" new school. A young boy became very excited when he found that the "new school" was really at the "end of the street, just where it is supposed to be."

When children move from one school to another as a group, and when they move from one home to another, there is a sense of loss and sadness. I think the sense of loss is a kind of re-creation of their original loss of mother during their weaning period. When children have to give up something that gives them comfort and a feeling of satisfaction, there is a sense of anger associated with this loss. The anger may be seen and felt by mother as such things as even biting the nipple if they are breast fed, or refusal to suck — a refusal to do the very thing that they want to do. This anger is experienced by some mothers as a sense that their baby is upset, "He's different now, maybe he's just growing up," or, "He has some trouble falling asleep now." They have been unable to recognize that the upset feeling is anger and is associated with a sense of loss.

## 40. Separation and Loss (in Later Life)

I do not think that separation and loss are problems of children or young adults alone. While not much has been written about the effects of separation and loss on older people, it is certainly a very significant part of their daily lives. Since they are older, peers and siblings are of an age when they are often ill and dying, in a real sense, and about to leave them. It is not only the death of friends and family that leaves older people suffering loss. It is also having to leave homes where they have been living for many years.

One such incident that was brought to my attention involved an older woman, over eighty years, who had moved from her apartment to a new apartment in another town where her daughter lived. She prepared for the move over several months and finally moved with belongings she wished to keep. The move seemed uneventful except for a complaint that soon developed. She felt "claustrophobic" in her new apartment (one-bedroom, living and dining room, kitchen, hall and bathroom) which she said was "very small" and made her feel "like she was trapped." From someone who had visited with her in her former apartment, I discovered that her former apartment was a very small "bachelor" flat (simply one room with a bathroom) without a view out her single window. Her new apartment looked out on a vista through large windows in both bedroom and living room. It also had a walk-out to a patio, something she thought she had always wanted. I think her experiencing of loss in reaction to the change occasioned the "claustro-phobia." This was her way of dealing with her feelings of separation and subsequent anger. Unfortunately, the reaction was accompanied by a painful hip problem that could only be relieved by rest. After four weeks in her new apartment, she felt her new place was fine and as good as her old one and the pain in her hip was somewhat relieved. As she moved about, she explained that she felt better when she was doing something and that her hip was not painful everyday. I think the pain will gradually subside but reappear whenever she feels the loss of her old place and the anger of having made a change, even though she was sure that she wanted to make this move.

Even though we consciously decide about a change, we still have a reaction to it. It is very important to acknowledge our human responses to change. I think this will make us more accepting of other people's reactions to separation as well.

## 41. Grief and Mourning

When a child's parent or an important relative dies, grief and mourning become part of that child's life as well as part of the parent's life. It is so important at these times to be able to tolerate the feelings of the child along with the intense feelings the adults have. It is important to help the child express these feelings and not "bury" them. To be alone at such a time is cruel to a child — abusive in fact. It is urgent that a child in mourning be with someone who can tolerate the child's pain and loss. Time-in at such times is vital and could be said to be every child's right.

Maya, a five-year-old, responded to the announcement that her grandfather had died with "lets go out and have some ice cream." Her parents were astonished that she would say this when they knew how close she was to her grandfather. They became very angry with her and lectured her about "feelings" when someone dies. Her quiet response to them after they finished their lecture was "I was afraid that if I cried you would get even more upset."

Romi, an eight-year-old, told his parents that he didn't care that his aunt had died: "She wasn't very nice and she smelled." His parents became very upset and sent him to his room "to learn not to say such bad things." Romi went to his room and broke all his "constructions" — his airplane models. When his father asked why he did this Romi replied "I needed to punish myself because I am very bad."

If the parents recognized that these children needed to have "safe" time-in with their parents and understood their words as their reactions to intense feelings, then both the children and their parents might have had an easier time dealing with the death of a loved one.

Parents, even though they are distressed by the death of someone close to them, need to know that they should remain close to their children. Children imagine that, since a relative died, their own parents may die, and they need to be reassured that their parents are well and capable of handling not only their own feelings, but those of their children. Children will deny the death of a relative, will become angry or will behave as if the death doesn't matter to them, when actually, they are worried about their own parents' health. Reassuring them and making them feel safe will enable them to express their emotions of grief and mourning.

## 42. Dealing with Crises

A friend, a young woman with two children, was rushed to the emergency room and did not have any time to prepare her children, aged two and six, for her departure. It was not until the next day that her children were able to visit her, and although their father had tried to comfort them, they remained anxious and distraught about being separated from their mother. Speaking with the mother early in the morning before the children were to arrive it was clear that by now she was feeling much better and was obviously on the mend. Her concern was that she be able to accept the children's anxieties and allow them to express their feelings about being separated and "left alone" for the night — not only being upset, but maybe angry.

I suggested that she ask her husband to bring crayons, pencils and paper with him when he brought the children. After greeting the children — and because sometimes when children are separated from a parent for even a short time, they often feel that the parent is angry with them or they are angry with the parents, or both — I suggested she encourage them to make drawings of the hospital room. The suggestion was to allow the children to select whatever they were attracted to and draw that. This would give their mother the opportunity to help the children ask questions about what they were drawing and during this questioning she could encourage them to talk about their feelings and concern about finding their mother in a hospital room. I suggested that she tell the children how she was feeling physically, that her voice was stronger now as she was feeling much better and that she would be home in a few days. However, they would have visits with her before she went home and they would be able to see how strong she was getting. I felt it was important for the children to not only realize that they had nothing to do with her emergency hospital admission but also that she was not "sick." Rather, she would try to help them to see that she had a problem which needed the hospital to help her, that the hospital was helping and she was getting stronger every minute. Soon she would be strong enough and would be able to leave the hospital.

When the children arrived they were upset, anxious and at times avoidant of their mother. They clung to their father as he held the crayons and paper. As their mother talked to them, telling them how her voice was getting stronger, how she was getting stronger and how much she missed not seeing them tucked into bed last night, they warmed and approached her side. She did not make any quick moves to scoop them up, although that is how she felt, giving them the time to adjust to the strange new feelings they were experiencing and to the strangeness of seeing their mother in a hospital room. As they approached her, she encouraged them to come in close to her. They all hugged each other with mother telling them that she missed them as much as they missed being with her. She said she knew their father had crayons and paper and perhaps they wanted to draw some of the things that they noticed in the room.

It is interesting that they took the crayons and paper and at first concentrated on distant things, like the door wall, gradually moving in on the object that was most important to them, their mother in bed. As they drew their drawings, mother and children were able to engage in a lively conversation — at first about the "outside" and what it was like; then about the door, the bed and what was beside the bed; then about mother in the bed. The questions about what, why, when, how long came quickly and the drawings and scribbling continued with the activity serving as a vehicle for conversation. Children, and adults as well, are able to talk more when they are "doing" something. Perhaps it is the activity, but probably it is that they are making concrete, aspects of a difficult, complex, if not abstract world that is just too intricate and intense for them to relate to. When they draw it, they select and can concentrate on what is important to them while leaving out all those other bits and pieces that sometimes complicate feelings even more.

The visit went well, the children were able to leave with the promise of many telephone calls before the next visit. They wanted to know why mommy would not be home to give them lunch or tuck them into bed at night. Their mother responded that she would be thinking of them at lunch, and at bedtime and that they should phone her before lunch and bedtime and tell her what they were doing. Their mother also indicated, on a calendar, that there were two days before she would be home, again pointing out how much stronger she was feeling and how good it was to see her children. The children needed to be reminded of these nurturing things to make sure that their (inside) "good mommy" was not in danger of becoming a "bad mommy." Children have a difficult time holding onto good inside feelings when they are frustrated and upset. The mother took the opportunity of asking them to telephone her before important daily events and of letting them tell her what they were about to do.

I think it is essential that the parent not "whine" about, for example, how much the children are missed, how much better it is at home. All this does is reinforce the idea that the children are either not to enjoy themselves while the parent is in hospital, or that the parent, in some fantastic way, is blaming the children for being in hospital. Neither way is alright. Rather, the parent should be able to let the children talk about what they want to talk about, to encourage their questions and to never make children feel they are responsible for the sickness.

Before the visit the children were becoming irritable, frenetic so to speak, not able to settle to anything and seemingly always under foot. The father had a lot to do. He had to juggle his work, the house and the needs of his wife, to say nothing about the needs and demands and worries of the children. His own anxieties interfered with his parenting in that he kept trying to get the children to be calm, not to worry, "mommy was fine, they would see her soon." None of this was of much help. The children continued to be irritable and at first his reaction was to send them to their rooms where they would be "at least out of sight." Fortunately, when he spoke to his wife, they decided together that the children's upset was due to their concern about not seeing their mother, and sending them to their room would only suggest that they were a nuisance and that their worries were not real. In no way could these young children cope with the worries they were having by themselves. They could not adjust to these concerns nor adapt to this event by themselves. They needed their father's patience and understanding and that is just what he next gave them — a time-in with him to help calm them and to become prepared for their first visit to the hospital, a visit that was being anticipated by their mother as well.

A time-out during a crisis only adds to the child's sense that whatever is not working that "used to work okay before" has made "me bad enough to send away." There is a considerable confusion that is experienced by the child during a crisis. Being upset because a parent is not there is also experienced very concretely by the child as a pain, literally a physical pain, and a mounting sense of panic. To imply to the child that she can cope with this confusion, the sense of panic and the physical pain is too much for most if not all children. As adults we do not want to be alone when we are terribly upset. Why should children? It is perhaps our own sense of impotence, of not being able to know how to help children, that forces us to send them away at just the times when they need us most and must be able to count on our strength to help them through the crisis.

## 43. Patterns of Development

When thinking about the development of a young child, we need to consider the way in which the child progresses. Progress is not made all at once, nor is it made in all areas of development at the same time. This might almost be saying a very well known truism except for the fact that I have talked to so many parents who are concerned when the "control" their child was showing "a week ago" is seemingly suddenly lost.

First, take the example of an eleven-month-old boy I know. He has been developing very well, actually starting to do that kind of walking often referred to as "cruising" — holding on to the coffee table with one hand and maneuvering his way around and around the table. With every rotation he seemed to do it just a little bit better. His parents praised him on and he responded to their loving reactions to his magnificent feats of walking. Next, he began to take his hands off the coffee table and to stand there as if suspended in space. Then, ever so casually and under control, he dropped down to the floor. He had mastered the difficult physical act of balancing alone, and then not falling, but actually sitting down. He was so happy — he burst out with smiles, chuckles and loud vocalizations.

His parents expected that he would move on to walking soon and he did within about one week. Having accomplished this major task, he then seemed to concentrate on sounds and repeating what seemed to be very special vocalizations. His walking did not stop along with his increased vocal activity but as his parents said, "He wouldn't let go of the coffee table, he wouldn't take any more steps by himself and in fact, he seemed to want to be held much more — suddenly he's a much younger baby." They seemed upset but, what was more concerning, disappointed in their baby's development, and considered that there might be something wrong with him. Describing their son's activities, they voiced these anxieties but centered on the idea that maybe they were not stimulating him enough — maybe it was their fault.

In discussions, I pointed out how this was not their fault, that there is a pattern to development followed by most children in which they move ahead in one area — that area of development is concentrated on — and nothing else seems to matter. The mother said "You mean that's why he was not as interested in food and eating as he had been before he went on his walking spree" when this observation was acknowledged. I asked her what happened after he began to look confident about his walking and she replied that she must not have had trouble feeding him, because she does not recall "food and eating as a big thing before."

Now he is concentrating on talking and communicating and his walking has taken a back seat. In fact, it seems less effective than it was just a week ago. I think it is less effective, but what usually happens is that within another week or so he will be able to vocalize "the way he wants" and then his walking will suddenly seem to jump forward. He will walk just as well and probably better than he did just before he showed an indifference to getting around by himself. While he was

dealing with this new and difficult task related to speech, not only did
his walking look "worse" but he was "off his food" and bedtimes were
difficult. He did not want to be by himself. In general, he seemed to let
go of those advances he had made in favor of concentrating on his
newly evolving facility of speech, but as he did so he needed more
time-in with his parents.

Often parents become very upset by what seems like a backward
step in development and have not supported their child when the child
needed their closeness. They have insisted that the child walk because
he walked before, that he eat because he is such a good eater and that
he also go to bed in the same way as he used to before these changes in
development occurred.

## 44. Eating

I have often wondered about parents who tell their children not to
stuff their mouth or criticize them when they seem to be saving some
small piece of food "until the last." When some children stuff their
mouth, usually to the despair of their parents, the children get smiles
on their faces and seem to look so contented and satisfied. I relate this
sense of satisfaction of a full mouth to the experience of warmth and
affection from mother. When your mouth is full of good food it is like
having a good enough mother fill you up. And the idea of leaving the
very best piece until the last is not just a child's idea of saving the best
to relish at the end. I see adults do the same thing — keeping themselves tantalized until the very end of the dish!

Perhaps it is to keep themselves interested in eating that people
keep the best piece of food for the last, but I think the meaning is a
little bit deeper than that. Perhaps it has something to do with managing one's emotions, controlling and maintaining control over feelings
— not just bad ones but good ones as well. We often complain that
children "just can't wait!" However, if a child saves the best piece for
last, then maybe the child is showing the capacity to delay gratification.

When parents put too much food on a child's plate and the child
becomes very picky and fussy, refusing to eat, saying she has too much
on her plate, this is, I think, "crowding." Children, as well as adults,

have difficulty when they are crowded and have to try and organize their space so they have some space for themselves. Putting too much food on a plate is "crowding" the child and the child's reaction is to become irritable. Put less food, give the different foods space between them and rely on children's hunger and sense of satisfaction to lead them to ask for more.

A pair of two-year-old boys were permitted to eat when they wanted to. They were encouraged to ask for food when they felt hungry and even though they had several snacks each day they participated in family mealtimes. The mothers of both boys were criticized and were told that their children would not only be picky eaters but that they were "spoiling" their children. With some support both mothers continued to follow their own advice, yet had some trouble with all the criticism they were getting — even from their own families!

Both children are now five-year-old, and both are excellent eaters. There are no feeding hassles and meals are usually a pleasurable time. The mothers are not worried that their children are not eating enough and both children are curious enough to taste all sorts of food. There were some beginning difficulties, for example, at times one of the children said he did not want to sit at the table with his parents. He was offered the kitchen counter and began to eat his food there, returning quickly to the table for fear that he might miss some talk that would be going on between his parents.

Control over food seems to represent control over feelings, and for children, this means that the concrete control over the food becomes representative of the concrete control over themselves. They can do things independently and are willing to try, yet they are also capable of asking for help when they see they need help. When the parent maintains control over food it is the same for the parent as the child, but now the parent has control over behavior. As one father said, "When I control the food, I can have some peace." It is too bad this father does not realize that what may seem like control right now will become a battle in a few months or years over who is in charge. The gain in control this father is getting right now may be offset by estrangement from his child in later years when there is a battle over independence and being in charge of oneself.

At first just such a problem was happening to a two-and-a-half-year-old girl. While the parents managed the food and told her she could not eat between meals because she'd lose her appetite, she began to smear her feces. The parents were very upset at this change in their daughter from a neat, clean little girl to a smearing, messy child almost overnight. The problems usually occurred at night. She would have a bm, put her hand in her diaper and smear the bm over her crib, herself, the wall — whatever she could touch. When the parents asked for help, I suggested they make food and eating less restrictive and that foods be given freely and especially whenever the child asked for any foods. The parents were very concerned about the smearing, but this concern seemed to be overridden when they asked, "Won't we spoil her if we give in to her demands?"

I told them that food and satisfaction would not spoil her but it was interesting that while smearing was definitely upsetting to them, it seemed, at least at this time, to take second place to spoiling!

As they talked about food, spoiling and satisfaction, I also recommended that they give her puddings to eat — but puddings which she could freely smear over her high chair and even herself if she wanted to and that they not put her out of sight when she did this. I also suggested that they allow her to taste the smeared puddings. The parents wondered if this would not encourage her to taste her bm but I pointed out that we did not know whether she was doing this already because she did have feces on her face. With a sense of disgust, annoyance and despair, they agreed to allow her to use the puddings in this way if she wanted to. She is now three-year-old and there are no smearing problems, either with the bm or the puddings. The feces smearing stopped within a couple of weeks.

A four-year-old boy seems to sum up the issue of food, feeding, mother and father, control and freedom in this conversation with his mother:

Mother:    Do you have a mommy inside of you?
Teddy:      Yes.
Mother:    Is it a good mommy or a bad mommy?

Teddy:    A good mommy.

Mother:   What does she do?

Teddy:    She gives me her nipple to suck when ever I need it.

(And at this point he slipped his thumb in his mouth and began to suck.)

### 45. Play

Sometimes parents are concerned about how often or how much they should play with their baby or young child. Parents may recognize that often the child does not need a parent to play with him but does need a response to statements or activity to prevent their play from becoming stale. While mother and baby are quiet, with the baby playing and the mother watching, the baby will quickly become engrossed in play. After a few minutes, mother's comment on the play enables the baby to become more involved and more engaged in the play. The theme of the play does not change, no new toy is introduced into the play and the mother has not moved from her spot. She simply talks to her baby, commenting on the play after the baby has been playing for a short while.

Parents often become "too involved" in their baby's play. They bring in too much, make rather inappropriate suggestions, take over the play and try to teach how to do something when the baby is engrossed in another aspect of the play or is not yet ready for their suggestions. In many ways parents may over-stimulate or stimulate inappropriately. Babies need their parents to watch what is going on, to let the activity develop for a bit and then comment on what has been going on — not what is going to happen. Comments do not require either new materials to be brought in, or a change in the activity theme.

I find many parents seem disappointed by the play their child is involved in, thinking that it is "too low level" or that the play needs "a change of direction." Usually, neither is effective. If the play is changed, the child will leave the activity altogether. The child may just throw the toy away and start to cry or just sit there without trying to do anything.

None of these result in adequate development of play behavior. Parents who get angry with their children when they do not follow their directions or instructions — might consider that their recommendations are too far in advance of the play or too interfering. Young children will balk at their interventions. They are creating a situation where the children will not as yet have the confidence to try things on their own. Neither of these effects is desirable. It is best to not get annoyed, not change the theme of the play, not add anything into the play but rather to sit there, be attentive and observant, comment every now and then and give the children enough time to respond. Children are not as quick to reply as we might expect. If given enough time, most children will reply — either through vocalization or action or both, — whether they are playing or just looking at the parent.

## 46. When to Provide Support (and When to Wait)

We have to ask ourselves what can we expect our child to do alone and when should we step in to help her with her problems and difficulties? We have to know when we should handle the difficulty for the child and when we help the child to deal with it with our help. This means that we try to create the kind of relationship where we will let the child test her own resources, competencies and strength. To do this the child needs to know that the parents not only care about what happens, but can offer their confidence for her to do something on her own.

When Timmy started to walk around the coffee table, his parents cleared the route. They made the corners and edges safe by putting soft plastic around the sharp edges of the table. They set the scene so that their baby would be able to walk without dangerous edges and corners. They put cushions in what they considered to be strategic spots and then they encouraged him to walk. Parents need to give their children a chance to try things out but they need to clear the way so that this can be done safely.

Sometimes parents think that there is not enough time to let the child experiment and even practice their new and emerging developments. In the case of Sasha, who was learning how to feed himself, his parents did not seem to have the time to let their son do things for himself. They did not want him to be "too messy" nor to take too long to eat and so they usually fed him while he played with one of his toys. When he tried to grab for the food, they stopped his hands or made a face saying "that's dirty" or "don't touch." Soon Sasha did not try to interfere and his parents felt they were doing a good job because there was so much more time to play with Sasha now that mealtimes were over so quickly. Unfortunately Sasha developed an "eating problem." At first he only wanted certain foods, like bananas. Then he "went off bananas" and only drank milk. He soon stopped drinking milk and would not eat at all. He simply closed his mouth and turned his head away from the spoon. This fifteen-month-old baby was reacting to his parents' demands for quickness and cleanliness by not eating at all. In a way, it is much faster if you do not eat at all!

Babies need to try to feed themselves. They need to play with the food. Sometimes they even need to try to feed their parents. They use their special spoons in ways that are spoon-like. At other times they act like these are not spoons, but combs to be run through their hair! It is probably more difficult for the parent to let these things happen but then these are children who are not apt to have eating problems.

I think there are times when a child should be able to dawdle over food, messing or picking things up. Sometimes this happens when the parent is in a rush. Parents have to realize how much their child can be rushed without creating an event fraught with tension. Parents will realize that they've been rushing their children when they find that they just will not try things, they immediately balk at frustration, cry easily or wait for things to be done for them. These children do not participate in "doing." Rather, they wait for their parent to do whatever is necessary. These children's concern about doing things makes them see themselves as "not being able" and they quickly stop doing things that create a sense of anxiety. The anxiety is just too difficult for them to endure and it seems safer for them to behave as if they cannot do whatever has been causing them the anxiety.

Lucy had been very interested in piling blocks one on top of another into many low piles and would spend hours doing this. The blocks often fell down but Lucy, a four-year-old, was interested in choosing blocks, not in replacing them or rebuilding the pile. This is what her father wanted her to do. After a few days of his interaction Lucy stopped her play with blocks. She left a favorite activity because it became too much for her to cope with her father's interference.

## CHAPTER 7

# ABOUT CHILDREN WHO GROW UP WITH "TIME-IN"

### 47. The Importance of Taking Risks

Without the opportunity to take a chance, and I mean take a chance within safe boundaries, then children's thinking and behavior will become repetitive and similar, and lacking in individuality. Divergent thinking and problem-solving will not emerge and only a few children will dare to do something difficult or different from their friends.

Since intelligence is made up of many different aspects and not simply one "thing" then I think we limit children's intellectual development if we stop them from taking risks and exploring, especially if they have to operate under externally imposed standards and adult expectations too early. Nor should we put the same standards on children of different ages. Some children will manage to adjust to adult standards, but certainly not all. Age and emotional maturity will often determine who can adjust and whether the cost of such adjustment will mean a self that does not take risks.

Children will worry that they are failing their parents when expectations for them are so much more than they can tolerate. When they are told "no more of your lip," "no more of that saucy attitude," "no more babyish ways" when they are not yet capable of maintaining these standards, children become fearful of trying new strategies. They stick to solutions that seemed to work in the past, and have some difficulty in recognizing that a new approach is needed. Their creativity is limited when this happens. It is important that the adult find some of the thinking and behavior of their child to be of "value" and that they let their child know this.

For example, a parent told his child, "Thank you for helping me put the vegetables and fruit away. When you want to put the six apples in the bin at once, you might try to carry them over to the fridge in a bag, not loose in your arms." The parent acknowledges the "value" of the help the child has shown as well as the source of the problem when the six apples spilled all over the kitchen floor.

Criticism without anger and resentment enables the child to understand the criticism without limiting his attempts at creating ingenious ways to do things.

## 48. Fear of "Falling Apart"

It is especially important that children have time-in during that time when they cannot do "things" alone and/or cannot experience emotions alone. Young children need the added protection of their parents' confidence and competence, their sense of strength and parenthood — their self — to be helped through fleeting periods of distress or crisis. As the parent loans their strength, their children gain confidence. Rather than being "spoiled," as is so often predicted, the next time these children have these feelings, or experience these events, they will try to handle it themselves. Their sense of inner strength and optimism comes from knowing they will be able to go to mother or father without feeling as if they have failed or disappointed them. They need not "fall apart" attempting to meet or pass a standard for which they are not yet ready. The children's selves are actually strengthened by the parents' presence. While with the parent, children can take the risk of exploring their feelings (of failure) because at such times the anxiety of "falling apart" is much reduced. Based on their previous experience, these children know the parent will just not allow this to happen.

Often, another very important gain is made. Simply by anticipating that "my parent will be there" or "I can go to my parent," the stress of an event is reduced. The fear of failing or disappointing (self or parent) is less since the child knows, "I can be with my parents; I feel sufficiently strong to try by myself — I'm prepared to try." A sense of independence built upon time-in with parents, on the willingness of parents to allow their child to depend upon them, enables the child to strive for this independence.

There is also a striving to be with parents. As difficult as it might be for them, children try to gain this time-in with their parents. Three-year-old Terry was busily kneading play-dough with her twin sister and a visiting friend of the same age. Each girl had a different color of play-dough and kept to a different section of the table. Their mothers chatted and kept an eye on the peaceful scene. Suddenly a piercing scream shattered the serenity of the moment and a pitched battle broke out over the use of a rolling pin. Terry's mother tried to umpire the scene and told Terry the guest should be able to have the rolling pin first. This upset Terry so much that she flung the play-dough and everything else on the table toward the wall of the room and proceeded to have a full-blown temper tantrum. Her reaction seemed out of proportion to anything that had been going on.

Terry's mother then took her by the arm and dragged her to her room, stating that she, Terry, needed time to think over what she was doing and how she needed to share things with guests. In the meantime, Terry was yelling so hard that she did not hear a word her mother was saying. When she was put in her room, she sobbed so intensely her whole body shook. She kept coming out of her room until finally her mother got the message: she did not, and could not, benefit from being by herself in her room. She needed to be close to somebody, to be held by somebody and to be told she was safe. Whatever brought on the excessive tantrum evidently scared the "wits" out of her and to be left on her own became even more scary to her because no one was there to help her. Once she sat on her mother's lap for a while, almost forcing her mother to hold her tightly, the sobs became softer, subsided, and Terry was able to join the others. She kept an eye on her mother and it took about a half-hour before she relaxed and played as before.

Terry needed, and was asking for, a return to her sense of attachment to her mother; she needed the support of her mother to go through the extreme emotional reactions she was experiencing. She needed a re-creation of her original attached state, including the security, warmth, smells and touch of a safe mother. She needed the re-creation of a sense of being contained and made to feel safe from her intense feelings even though neither she nor her mother really knew why these feelings were expressed. Certainly, at this time she did not "need" her mother to be angry with her or to put her out of sight. When Terry was given the safety and support of time-in she was gradually able to regain a sense of competence, a sense of her own internal control. However, the strength of whatever Terry had been feeling that lead to her "falling apart" took a half-hour to subside. Sometimes, we not only fail to recognize the need children have to be with adults, but we also do not recognize just how long it takes to get over an upset and to re-establish a sense of inner equilibrium.

It is during that time when Terry did not feel able and competent to be alone that she needed the protection and warmth of her parent's strength, her mother's ego, to help her through a difficult, and short period of time. When a child becomes so frightened or so upset that she cannot get through the time alone, she needs the time-in with her parent to regain her usual composure.

"Loaning" our strength, that is our understanding, acceptance and recognition that the feelings are too strong to endure alone, gives a child like Terry the sense of confidence, our sense of confidence, that, with help, she can get through a difficult period. The sense of confidence that is gradually shared between child and parent helps the child accept the risk of trying to handle the difficult feelings on her own next time. Since this parent was able to help her child through the difficult emotions she was experiencing, the child was reinforced in the feeling that "I can try it on my own the next time." Rather than giving up and having a tantrum in the future, the child *is more* likely to come to the parent for support and/or try to handle the situation alone. If the situation and the feelings become too difficult then the child is likely to try and find the parent for some help, essentially for time-in.

## 49. Growth of the Capacity for Empathy

Social development includes the ability to be sensitive to others, to empathize or "read" other people's feelings. I think children will not be able to do this accurately unless parents *read their children's feelings accurately*, sometimes by identifying strong feelings in their children and/or by asking them how they feel when they can answer. Parents also have to be honest about *their own* feelings when their children ask them in turn.

Too often I have heard children being unable to judge others' feelings because whenever they said to their parents, "You're angry," the parents have denied these feelings even though they actually were angry. These parents said they did not think they should tell their children how angry they were because it might "frighten" the children. Sometimes they did not know themselves that they were angry. Generally these parents felt that their children did not need to know how they felt, they just needed to know what to do! The ability to predict and understand others' feelings rests upon important "others" telling you that you are right when you have accurately identified the emotion. Denying what is obvious to the child leads children to distrust their own judgments and gradually to not try to understand others or even themselves. These children seem to go from reaction to reaction, as if looking for ways that they can "really" tell what's happening. So some of these children actually create events in order to "blow-up," because then "you really know how to read your parents!" It is unfortunate that some children are driven to this extreme only to be told that they have to go into their bedrooms and stay there — until they learn that they're not allowed to recognize such intense feelings in parents.

## 50. "Knowing It All"

A four-year-old boy I know would always say "I know" to anything that was said or asked. He knew it all! When told about the "rules," he said, "I know." When an event or a situation was described to him, he said, "I know that." He persisted with "I know" until at one point he was asked a question about the sky and clouds. He very angrily said, "If you tell me then I'll know!" When told the answer to the question, he said he knew that! This young boy needed to know everything. I think he was demonstrating his sense of self-control by knowing everything. When he had a grip on his sense of control over himself, I did not hear "I know" anymore!

In a similar way, babies about nine to twelve months begin to shake their heads "no" to just about everything their parents ask them or tell them. When being fed they shake their head "no." When asked if they want a toy, even a favorite one, they shake "no." Often, parents describe this behavior as "strange," "cute," or as "I don't know what this means." I think this means the very beginnings of self-control where the baby is trying to internalize the idea of "no." The baby is saying "no" to himself. The baby is beginning to develop a sense not only of who he is but what feelings need to be under his control. The idea that the baby *cannot* have everything he wants whenever he wants it is becoming part of himself. I do not mean that the baby does not want the food, or the toy, rather, the baby is practicing the idea of being able to have a sense of inner control later on. The child is developing a sense of self-control.

## 51. The Development of Self-Control

Parents are often worried their children will not develop self-control and quickly impose ways they consider will help children develop this control. Thinking that children are helped to develop this elusive quality by being alone and thinking about why they are "wrong" or "bad," parents will use the time-out method. However, from the child's point of view, the idea of considering yourself sufficiently bad that you need to be banished is difficult. If this feeling is combined with a sense that the parents are retaliating in response to your "badness" (by sending you out of their sight), then the feeling of badness can become exceedingly powerful. Some children respond to this approach by thinking they are so bad that nothing will ever save them from their fate of "being bad." These children take on a self-control that is characterized by self accusation and self reproach. They consider that everything they do will be "no good," that there are things they have done in the past for which they must apologize and that their future is expected to be very bleak because they will not be worthy of the nurturing they so desperately need.

These children feel guilty and often they try to do too much to make up for some unknown thing they think they did. However, children quickly come to their own conclusions when they think they did something wrong and "discover" what it is — it is *any event that occasioned angry feelings in them.* So, if going to bed seemed too early for the child and the child feels angry (as most children will), then going to bed "becomes a problem." The child has a difficult choice. Either she wants to go to bed early (which occasionally happens) or she anxiously tries to make sure that all the things she thinks she needs to do before bedtime are done. Rarely can these things be done to the child's satisfaction and so the parent eventually says that the child is "dawdling." This increases the child's anxiety because once again she begins to feel angry and she is not supposed to have angry feelings. The cycle develops in a very repetitive, almost compulsive, way of finding things to do before going to sleep because going to sleep means lying in the dark and thinking about the bad person you are. Going to bed is now a routine to avoid. This child is not being "wilful," she is trying to avoid the feelings of badness which will be felt when she is alone. This is a child who has developed a sense of self-control, to control very angry feelings. However, the sense of self-control is experienced as a sense of self reproach, because nothing that the child has done has resulted in an abatement of these feelings of anger. The child has not been able to accomplish any effective reparation for the feelings of anger.

Of course, not all children respond to parents this way. Some tend to ignore their parents and have constant arguments about "growing-up and being able to look after yourself." This sense of self-control is something that comes about as a very normal aspect of growing up in a supportive family environment and I see such "cheeky" children as having less difficulty with overpowering feelings of self reproach later.

While parents are able to see that their children's feelings are just too strong for them to handle by themselves, they can help by becoming the "container" for these emotions for a little while. One nine-month-old child was waking once during the night to nurse but then began to wake up twice, even three times a night. The parents wondered what was wrong and at first tried to respond as they had when he awoke only once. However, the baby did not respond well to this same feeding pattern and soon the parents had to figure out something else to do. Nothing seemed to work, at least not for more than one evening. Together they decided that their baby was growing up and that she just did not know what she needed or wanted at that moment. Rather than let her cry herself back to sleep, they would contain her sense of being uncomfortable by being with her, cuddling her, making her feel safe and helping her go back to sleep. Their idea was a simple one. They felt their daughter could not respond by herself to her sense of tension. So they decided they would be there for her when she needed them. They were tired for a few evenings, but gradually, within a week, the baby resumed her usual sleeping pattern and did not awaken several times each night.

Self-control is gained gradually and is not something that we can arbitrarily impose upon a child. The way children control themselves, either by trying to blame all the problems on mommy, daddy, brother or sister, or by blaming themselves for all the problems, is so often dependent upon the way we respond to our children. Too much parental control at too early an age makes the child a worried child and one who either succumbs to guilt or blames others.

We can expect our children to accept self-control if we recognize their need to be able to hand over some control to parents, and for parents to set boundaries that are in keeping with the child's level of growth and maturity. Too strict boundaries makes for fewer opportunities for the child to explore. Too lenient boundaries makes for a child who is searching for the boundaries and often misbehaves to find the limits.

By providing the child with our "supportive self," we create trust within this relationship. This trust nurtures the child's curiosity, the desire to take risks and explore and especially the capacity to begin to recognize when things are not going well and when the child needs to come closer to the parent. It facilitates the growth of the capacity for the child to tolerate change because the child recognizes that she can be with the adult should things get too tough or dangerous. This means the child can tolerate the idea of making a mistake and that she will not suffer rejection but gain support and help. When the adults give support and then praise, the child responds with more "grown-up behavior." Rather than having to push for more mature behavior, this child accepts this role as her maturity enables her to do so. She is not afraid of growing up.

## 52. The Capacity to Create "Reverie"

It is very important to recognize that most children have the capacity to create a "reverie" for themselves. By this I mean a thought or a feeling of being kept safe by the parent. Children have sometimes told me that when they are upset they think about times when they were safe as younger children with a safe parent or safe, known adult. Their reverie can be thought of as an attempt to recreate the time when they did not have to handle all their difficulties themselves. This "reverie" is essential for the development of self-control.

Children who are rejected or who are told to handle their problems on their own do not seem to have this ability to think about themselves as safe. Rather they view the world as dangerous and their parents as difficult. The very children who get into so much trouble, then, do not have the capacity to work their way out of the problem by remembering, by imagining themselves to have been safe with accepting parents. These children, six-, seven-, eight-year-olds, have no recourse but to "try" their parents again, that is to try to gain some sense of safety from them. But all too often these children find that once again their parents are not there for them. These children, I think, will be those adolescents who will have to find some way to make themselves feel safe in their own minds. They will have to create a "reverie" that makes them feel that they can carry on, and all too often this reverie will be created by using drugs or alcohol.

I think that parents must create an adequate boundary for the child, that is, the sense of an adequate container for the child's feelings. This is essential when the feelings are too powerful or intense for the child to experience by himself. If parents do not create this container then the child needs to try and construct something outside of himself to prevent massive anxiety from disintegrating the child's sense of self.

We all know some babies who seem to go to pieces when they are undressed, or have their face washed or when their feed is interrupted. These babies show a restlessness, a lot of uncoordinated movements of their limbs, and crying or even screaming. If these babies are contained, that is, not totally undressed for a bath, but given a sponge bath while covering up the part that is not being sponged, or carried about in a comfortable and close way, or even fed close to the parent, these babies respond with reduced distress and easier interaction with their parents. This containing by the parent makes for a feeling of coherence — a sense of being held together.

This sense of being held by another, the sense of being understood, of being thought about, of being contained, helps us when we are older when we need to have something, some thought or feeling to hold onto when we are under stress or tension. Essentially, this time-in with our parents serves us throughout our lifetime. These time-ins enable us to reflect upon, to have a reverie of, safe, contained times with a trusted, responsive adult. We can then approach our problems with understanding and perspective.

# CHAPTER 8

# QUESTIONS AND ANSWERS

These are some of the questions I received from parents when I gave talks about time-in, and when I was interviewed about time-in for *Today's Parent* Magazine in 1993 and 1995.

Q. I'm a working parent and I've read a lot about how important "quality time" is. What is the difference between "quality time" and "time-in"?

A. I'm not sure what you've read or heard about "quality time." It is often used to refer to the nature of the time parents spend in "face to face" interaction with their children, as opposed to the amount of time spent together doing chores or other "household" activities.

"Time-in" is most certainly "quality time." It is a parenting strategy and style for helping children who are experiencing episodes of emotional, behavioral or developmental stress by staying with them while you resolve the feelings together. It encompasses the feelings and behaviors parents express when their children are "out-of-control."

So often parents plan an outing, say to the park, which they anticipate will be pleasurable. To their dismay, their child might not want to leave the swings to feed the ducks, or hurls the apple juice out of the stroller, or screams because there is mud on his shoes. The parent feels that the "quality time" has been spoiled and takes the child home in disappointment and anger.

Taking "time-in" to resolve those expectable moments of fussing on outings allows both parents and children to carry on with the excursion without feeling that it has been "spoiled." "Time-in" is practicable anywhere, anytime. "Time-in" parents recognize that their child's moods and needs will not adapt to parental agendas. Children will have moments of difficulty regardless of how much fun they are having — in fact, maybe, because of it!

Children react with strong emotions to parental expectations and feelings, whether they are stated and often special occasions and holidays are both stressful and pleasurable.

Q. I have a three-year-old daughter who gets out of control when she can't have her own way. This is an especially difficult problem when the things she wants to do are too hard for her, like tie her shoe laces or pour a drink from a full pitcher. I have tried "time-in" by talking to her and telling her that she can't always do what she wants rather than sending her to her room, but she just seems to get angrier and starts to hit me and yell.

A. You are to be commended for not sending your daughter to her room when she is angry with you and for trying to help her sort out what she can and cannot do. This is a confusing and difficult task for children of this age, who often have very strong and clear ideas about their wants and abilities. An important part of "time-in" is the way you respond to this need of hers to explore her sense of herself. It might be helpful to ask yourself whether the things she wants to try are really unreasonable, or otherwise unacceptable to you, and whether you have helped her to understand this at a time when she is not upset.

If you are content that you and she understand the "rules," then quietly sit with her when you have to say "no" to a demand and she becomes angry with you. I would suggest that you tell her that you are very proud of the many things she can do — perhaps remind her of some of them — and recognize her anger and frustration at you and at the limitations you are imposing. Perhaps you could suggest an alternate activity, or talk with her about other ways to do the thing you think she wants to do. By giving her a chance to explain her demands, you might find that she has something entirely different in mind from what you thought.

It is important not to "be angry" through body language or tone of voice when having "time-in" with your child. If you seem irritated or frustrated, she will react to your manner, even if you say that you are not angry. When children are upset, angry words or behaviors will trigger more anger and guilt in them. Even sitting too close, or talking too much, can also be problematic for some children.

Testing abilities against wishes and limits is a task that continues throughout childhood and into adolescence. Children will do this repeatedly as they grow, and as you change your rules and expectations to conform with changes in them. Constantly re-negotiating this is a built-in way of ensuring that parent and child remain up to date with each other. Using "time-in" to discover creative solutions that suit both you and your child will stand you in good stead in the coming years.

Q. I have a five-year-old child in day-care in the afternoons after he attends a morning kindergarten. The workers in the center are always using "time-out" with my son because they say he won't listen to them and he runs around without stopping. I don't like "time-out" because it seems to upset him, yet I see them using it all the time with him and with the other kids. The teachers in his morning program don't seem to have these problems with him. What can I do ?

A. It is regrettable that "time-out" is so widely used as a solution to behavioral problems in some child care facilities. I think that it is important for you to discuss this issue with the staff, pointing out that there seems to be a difference between his behavior in the morning and the afternoon. You may also want to observe in the day-care for a time to sort this out before asking for a meeting to share your concerns. He may be tired after a half day of kindergarten, or perhaps the routines and expectations are very different between morning and afternoon programs. I think he is reacting to the use of "time-out" in the afternoon, and his "excessive" running is an expression of his anger and anxiety created by the use of "time-out."

Q. My children are ten- and twelve-year-old and I am interested in what you have said about "time-in." I find your suggestions very appealing, but I'm afraid that it is "too late" to start. They're almost teenagers and everyone tells me that teens don't talk to their parents, no matter what you do. Won't they think it's odd if I try and talk to them now when there is a problem, whereas before I might have sent them to their rooms?

A. It's not too late — it' never too late! In fact, if you use "time-in" as your children approach adolescence, you will be able to set a pattern for a different way of relating that you will all find useful in the upcoming years. Despite the advice of your friends, many teens and their parents continue to talk openly during this time.

When you feel you "want" to send a child off to her room, instead invite the "offending" child to pull up a chair beside you. Talk calmly about what you see, how you feel and how you imagine your child might be feeling. Give her lots of opportunities to correct your perceptions and to share her feelings and thoughts with you.

Don't be surprised if your efforts are rebuffed at first — this will be new behavior for both of you, and your children may want to "test out" whether you will stay with them, or whether you are going to use time-out anyway. You may even hear sarcastic remarks like "what do you care" or "none of your business." This is normal and does not mean that your children are "rude" — they merely want to understand the new situation. Preteens and teens also often express themselves in ways that seem designed to provoke their parents. Their feelings are very intense and they are practicing expressing them. If you can remain calm in crises, and use "time-in," you will find that your children will soon create other opportunities to communicate with you, building on the confidence they gain through "time-in."

When your children reach puberty, and even in the few years before, you may notice that, at times, they seem more withdrawn and less willing to talk to you. That is why it is even more important to take "time-in" during periods of emotional upset, offering them every opportunity to let you know how they are feeling and what's on their mind. If they are sent to their room too many times then eventually you may not be able to get them out when you want to.

Adolescents, as much as younger children, need their parents' acceptance and understanding of their feelings and their moods. They are experiencing overwhelming moods and impulses that are frightening to them and your presence will reassure them that you are not scared and they are not "falling apart." They also need your help to develop a vocabulary to express themselves and your example during "time-in" is important in allowing this to emerge.

Teens and most children, however, react badly to what they feel is an interrogation or being "put on the spot." It is often helpful when having "time-in" with a teenager to do something together while you talk, such as preparing dinner or going for a walk. This lessens the likelihood that they will feel confronted. They also need time to think about their reactions, and may come back to you with thoughts or comments when you least expect it. Teens need a lot of space and "time-in" can be effective even if you only stay within earshot and allow them to approach you when they feel ready.

**Q.** My husband and I are at our "wits end" trying do deal with our four-year-old daughter who screams and tantrums a lot during the day or night, no matter what we do. She wakes up crabby, fusses about what to eat, what to wear and every little change and task seems to precipitate a crisis. We've tried being predictable and consistent. We've tried talking to her in advance of situations. We've tried everything, and she is just so "high energy" and "high need" that we are worn out. The only thing that seems to work to get her to do what she has to do as part of normal routines is "time-out."

If we have to take more time with her as "time-in" then we'll never get dinner made, or get out the door in the morning, and our older daughter will be completely neglected. As it is, she doesn't get as much help with her homework or as much attention as she needs. What can we do?

**A.** You've obviously been trying very hard to meet the needs of both of your children, with only some limited success. As you have pointed out, your younger daughter's behavior has not really changed over the long term, despite the "effectiveness" of the "time-outs." That is often the case with punishments like "time-out" or spanking — the effects are only very temporary because the rejection or the abandonment is so powerful that children often alter their behavior quickly and dramatically. Nevertheless, the original emotions have not been dealt with and new feelings of anger have been added with each use of "time-out," leading to a spiral of repeated episodes of difficult behaviors.

I would encourage you both to take "time-in" with your daughter even if you feel frustrated and tired. I think that you will find that you will not be spending excess amounts of time after the first few successful "time-ins," because your daughter will settle down as she anticipates your availability to soothe her emotions in a crisis. You will need to help her less frequently as she feels loved and accepted by you in crises.

Even managing "time-outs" is time consuming and disruptive, and the feelings of rejection and anger that your daughter is left with as a result of "time-outs" may even be provoking some of the outbursts the next day.

Q. What if my child tells me to "go away" or to "leave him alone" when he is having a tantrum? I've always thought that I should respect his wishes. What do I do?

A. I'm not sure how you and your son have handled tantrums in the past and what he expects you to say or do when he is having a tantrum. It is possible to stay nearby, perhaps sitting near him on the floor, or just outside the door, talking gently to him even though he doesn't seem to be listening to you. You can respect his wishes not to be "too close" by having "time-in" nearby, even if you are not sitting side by side. I would encourage you not to leave him completely alone despite his statements. He may just be worrying about how damaging his angry thoughts and feelings could be to you, or whether you could still love such an upset child.

What is important is that you "lend" yourself to him in a way that is experienced by him as accepting and non-judgmental. It may help to reassure him that you are not angry or upset with him for his tantrum, nor are you offended at being "sent away." You may have to "sit it out" with him a few times before he stops testing out whether you think he is so bad that he doesn't "deserve" to have you stay with him.

**Q.** I have a five-year-old girl who "goes crazy" every time I am going out and she has to stay with a babysitter. She seems happy and well adjusted at other times and goes to school easily. It's getting to the point where I dread going out because of the fuss. I've tried talking to her the day before to prepare her but this doesn't seem to help. She either ignores me or promises to be good when I go the next day, only to "melt-down" anyway. The problem is I can't take "time-in" with her at that moment because I am on my way out, and I don't want to be late. What should I do?

**A.** It sounds like you have started to try a "time-in" strategy by talking with your daughter before you go out, and this is a very good idea. Perhaps you and she can set aside some special time to be together for 15 or so minutes before you start getting ready to go out. You might allow her to stay with you while you are getting dressed, maybe even helping you select clothes. Talk to her while you are getting ready about where you will be going, who will be taking care of her and when you will return. You may also want to suggest that she draw a picture for you, to be waiting for you upon your return.

If she begins to get agitated during this "time-in" you can hug her and tell her that you love her, and that she and you both will be safe while you are away. You can reassure her that although you will be enjoying yourself while you are out, you will also be thinking about her, and that it is O.K. for her to have fun also.

She may still create a "scene" at the door and it might be a good idea to "allow" for five or so minutes for this in your scheduling. Again, you can hold her and tell her that she and you will both be O.K., and that you will return when she is asleep, or whenever suits the time of day. With your support in these "time-ins" she will gradually be able to manage the strong feelings she has when you leave her.

**Q.** I really agree with your suggestions about "time-in." I have never liked "time-out" for kids, but our family has used it for a toy instead! If my kids cannot agree to share, I put the toy in "time-out" until they have a plan that they both agree on for playing with it. What is your reaction to this idea?

A. You are to be congratulated for not using "time-out" with your children. I do think that expecting your children to agree on how to share a toy before playing with it, can be useful for developing cooperative skills, depending on the ages of the children. I would, however, avoid putting the toy in "time-out." The children will think the toy is "bad" and therefore has been rejected. It does not require a large leap of imagination for your children to put themselves in the place of the toy, and in their minds they may be worried that they will be "next."

Q. When I come home from work I look forward to seeing my kids but they seem to erupt into fighting and misbehavior as soon as I come through the door. I'm also tired and want a little space to change my clothes and settle in. I know everyone is hungry and needy, but "time-in" is the last thing I feel like having at that moment. Any suggestions?

A. I think that what you and your children are experiencing is very normal and common to many families. You are indeed right that everyone is tired, hungry, and "on the edge." There are no easy solutions for this time of day, however, most certainly, using "time-out" will make things worse. Children, understandably, want as much as they can get from their parents, especially after a long day apart. Parents want a little peace and quiet too!

It may be that you will "get a lot" by giving a little. By having an immediate "time-in" upon entering the house, in a focused way, the children will sense that you can, and will, be available to them, and you can absorb all of their immediate feelings. Then other issues can be dealt with as the evening progresses. The more you "fend them off," the more anxious and angry they will likely become.

It will be helpful to "fortify" yourself to do this by taking a few minutes for yourself before you get home, perhaps by having a cup of tea at a corner cafe. It will also help to tell the kids, as you are having "time-in" with them, that you are glad to be home with them, and that you are home for the evening (if you are). They will begin to develop a sense of confidence in your availability for them in those "opening moments" and throughout the evening, and their tensions will quickly subside. By the way, have a small snack prepared for the children that you can bring in during the "time-in."

**Q.** My five-year-old daughter just wants to do dangerous things — she climbs onto fences and walks along them as if she's on a tightrope. Just yesterday she climbed a telephone pole and then couldn't get down. I had to get the fire department to get her down. I've punished her by taking away privileges, by spanking her and by sending her to her room as a further consequence to let her know that she's doing some bad things. Nothing seems to work — what do you suggest?

**A.** You might want to enrol her in a gym class where climbing tight ropes, walking, balancing and other skills are taught. She may have a talent in that direction. Nevertheless, apart from enrolling her in a class, it does sound like she needs to be active and may, in fact, need more of your direction, caring and support on the spot! She might need you to help her recognize what is dangerous and what she can do.

Sending her to her room as a consequence of her behavior is not going to help her at all. In fact, it may only create a sense of anger and rejection in her. When she is sent to her room I'm sure she doesn't think that she has been bad even if you told her that — nor would a five-year-old think that mother was right to send her to her room to teach her not to do the bad deed. I have never spoken to a child who has been put in their room who has said that mommy or daddy put me in my room because they love me. Rather, these children have expressed resentment and do consider how to "get even." I think that these retaliation thoughts leave children with a feeling of guilt and worry that their parents will punish them for these thoughts — not for the reason they have been sent to their room. I think that children will behave badly later on in ways that seem unrelated to the original misbehavior because of the feelings they have when punished by "time-out."

With "time-in," you will talk to your child, telling her why she needs to be with you, why her behavior is dangerous and that she needs your support right now. Often the misbehavior is an attempt on the child's part to ask for your time, your support, your confidence in knowing how to handle situations. The child's time with you at those times reinforces the strength of the bond and enables her to call upon you when she needs you. The "time-in" situation leaves you both with good feelings towards each other.

Q. My eleven-year-old son has been misbehaving in class — he has suddenly become the class clown and doesn't seem to know when to stop his nonsense. We have tried to punish him by grounding him but that doesn't work. We know, and he also knows, that the school is about to suspend him from class. Is there anything we can do to help him?

A. Yes, I think there is. You might try to talk with him about his behavior. Tell him you are aware that it started recently and you don't know why he is doing this. Let him know that you want to be able to talk with him rather than punish him — and you might find that going for a car drive, just you and he, may help him to talk with you.

Punishing him won't work, as you are finding out! I think he feels angry or sad, resentful, humiliated and does not actually feel the remorse or think about how to make the changes his parents and teachers would like to see happening.

Grounding him or having him in "time-out" carries with it the expectation that he "will know better next time" — but it doesn't do that. I think it makes us think that the person doesn't like us, and the clowning in class may be his way of trying to actually hide the anxiety of being rejected and being angry. Punishment then seems to only reinforce the misbehavior, which actually may escalate, forcing you to punish him even more.

I think you need to have more time with your son. Try to find out what may be bothering him and try to look at the behavior from his point of view. He's trying to get something from the class; he's trying to become recognized; he's trying to find out what he can do to stand out and become an individual. These may be some thoughts he has. Our job as parents is to create a time with our children so that they feel comfortable, safe and free, loved and supported so that they can explore some of their thoughts about why they think they do what they do.

Q. My baby is seven-month-old and won't go to sleep by himself. I have to be in the room until he falls asleep. I've been told that he needs to learn to fall asleep by himself but if I'm not there he cries and cries and has even vomited because I didn't go to him. Is this O.K.?

A. No, I don't think so. I would not advise you to let your seven-month-old cry himself to sleep or cry until he vomits. All that you will do is prove to him that you are unavailable when he needs you. In order for babies to go to sleep "alone" they need to build up a sense of confidence in themselves that they can sleep, and fall asleep alone. In order to accomplish this they need their parents. By being with him and not letting him cry he gains the sense of confidence by your presence. If he is sufficiently important for you to be there, then he is sufficiently important to himself. It is the confidence in having parents there when you need them that gives you the sense of confidence in yourself.

So be there when he cries, have the same bedtime routine every night, don't excite him for at least an hour before you start the routine, and then, when you have him in bed and quiet, leave the room. If he cries come back and talk soothingly to him. If he persists then lift him and walk with him in his room. Try to put him in his crib again and only if he is alright leave the room. Of course you've made sure that he's not cold, hungry, wet, uncomfortable or sick, and if you've checked these, and any other possible problems then leave. If he cries again then repeat the soothing and walking process until he settles to sleep. You will find that within a short time, sometimes a week, he will go to sleep easily by himself.

What I am describing is "time-in" between you and your baby. Especially when he is upset, if you leave him to "cry it out," you leave him with time-out and I think that this only creates other behaviors which may be worse for him and you, rather than difficulty going to sleep.

Q. My daughter is very jealous of her new baby sister and no matter what I do I just can't stop her from trying to bite, scratch or hit her. She looks at the baby with such anger that it frightens me and she's only three-year-old. I've sent her to her room when she acts like that but she just comes back and does it again! What do you think

I should do?

A. I don't think you should send her to her room. That only makes her sense of being not wanted or rejected, stronger. You now have another daughter and sending your first to her room only reinforces the sense of being replaced — of not being wanted. She didn't ask for a sister; she thought she was all you wanted or needed and now she finds out she was not enough! You know — think about it — if your husband brought home another wife — of course you'd be angry and jealous. You would have to feel that he doesn't care for you any more or he wants someone else as well because you didn't "do" enough. Either way would make you angry.

Don't send her to her room. Do have her come and sit with you when she tries to hurt the baby or has hurt her. She needs to know you love and want to nurture her and that you have enough love and nurturing for both your children. Let her know that you know she's angry, but that you can't let her hurt the baby and that you will make it safe for both of the children. With time-in with your daughter you lend her your support and take care of her jealousy which she can't deal with by herself. She needs your strength at this time in her life.

Q. I've noticed that one of the students in my fourth grade class squirms a lot in his seat, especially when he has to do a short study test or answer some written questions I've given to the class. Is there some way I might help him to be able to sit quietly?

A. I think the student is communicating to you, in a body language way, he is uncomfortable, or at least, under some tension and pressure in trying to write out the answers to your questions.

I think that when children squirm in their seats they doubt their capacity to answer the questions and may actually begin to feel ill, like stomach aches or headaches.

Have the child come and sit beside you and read the question that is to be answered as you listen to his reading. What you are then helping him do is focus on the work rather than on the anxiety he is expressing. In my experience, I have seen children remain beside their teacher and begin to write their answers — yet without the squirming and physical discomfort. When the child begins to write you can talk to another "squirmer."

I think that the child's anxiety about doing well is just too great for him to endure alone. He needs you to act as his "container" by having "time in" with him; to let him know that you are listening to his reading, and then to enable him to remain close to you as he begins to write his answers. At that point he won't mind at all that you focus on another child. His anxiety will have been contained, and he will be able to go on with his work.